ENEMIES OF THE PEOPLE

WE'RE ALL SCREWED AND
HERE'S WHO TO BLAME

ENEMIES OF THE PEOPLE

SAM JORDISON

HarperCollins*Publishers*

HarperCollins*Publishers*
1 London Bridge Street
London SE1 9GF

www.harpercollins.co.uk

First published by HarperCollins*Publishers* 2017

1 3 5 7 9 10 8 6 4 2

© Sam Jordison 2017

Illustrations © Shutterstock.com

A catalogue record of this book is
available from the British Library

ISBN 978-0-00-825641-8

Printed and bound in Great Britain by
Clays Ltd, St Ives plc

CONTENTS

—

INTRODUCTION

———

Not too long ago, there was a fashionable theory that history was determined by economic and geopolitical forces rather than by individuals. Before that, the big idea was that Great Men governed history: that it took men (always men) of destiny, foresight, intelligence and strategic mastery to change the world and build the future.

But recent years have proved both those notions abundantly wrong. From Nigel Farage to Donald Trump via (inevitably) Vladimir Putin, our lives generally have been governed, endangered and thrown into confusion by a pack of angry men. (Nearly always men. Nearly always white.) Men whose ambition is inversely proportional to their ability – and stability. When was the last time you saw a decent leader outside of Canada? And when was the last time anyone in power did anything useful for you?* The truth is that most of the people who

———

* If you went to Eton with David Cameron, he probably did do plenty for you. But that doesn't count.

have guided our destiny have been far from great – no matter how often they might enjoy using that word.

And here we are, in 2017, post-truth and mid-Brexit. Nationalism is on the rise. A reality TV star is in the Oval Office. The UK is leaving the European Union and looks set to split apart. We are on the precipice of an uncertain future – and the people in this book are the ones who have stuffed us on the bus and driven us there.

Several of those listed are monsters. Not all. I have an uncomfortable feeling that Chris Martin may actually be quite sweet. But that's okay. *Enemies of the People* is not just intended as a roll-call of the evil, or even the unpleasant. Instead, the chapters are devoted to those who have helped us get to this dizzying and windswept cliff-edge, whether that be through malice, bad driving or accidentally taking a wrong turn.

So it is that there's no Attila the Hun, no Vlad the Impaler, not even Stalin. That's not to defend such ogres in any way – just to say that other people are currently at the wheel. If I were writing ten years ago, I would probably have included a very different set of names. In ten years' time we'll probably have a whole new bunch of worries.

But for now, *Enemies of the People* should be an interesting snapshot. True to our times, it was written quickly and in anger. I can't pretend to be objective. In fact, I can't pretend to be anything other than royally cheesed off. I've seen the world I love torn to shreds and I wish it hadn't happened.

But I have also tried to be true and to use verifiable facts. Because facts are important and facts endure. Which brings me to another big theory about history. They say it is always written by the victors. But at the moment, many of those victors can't seem to write more than 140 characters at a time. Which gives us a golden opportunity to set the record straight, to snatch back the narrative and to find a better road.

And if you want to win, the first thing you've got to do is to know your enemy.

ENEMIES OF THE PEOPLE

VLADIMIR PUTIN

—

Date of birth: *7 October 1952*
In a nutshell: *Ex-KGB hardman turned international puppet-master*
and bringer of chaos
Connected to: *Donald Trump, Nigel Farage, Marine Le Pen*

If Vladimir Putin had a better penis, life would be safer and kinder for all of us. As it is, the world's most obviously overcompensating politician has bare-torsoed himself into the history books by interfering in numerous elections, invading his neighbours, and corrupting political debate around the world … And that's before we even mention the way people who oppose him keep on having allergic reactions to bullets and poison.

Okay, we don't necessarily know that Putin has erectile disfunction. Plenty of biographies attribute his fondness for working out and chucking people around on Judo mats to the fact that he is just 5 ft 7 in. The theory goes that when Putin realised he was hitting puberty later than the other boys at his school and that they were outgrowing him, he decided that he'd have to learn some sick martial arts skills if he were to maintain his position as their chief bully* and tormentor.

Even so, there is something about all those photos his press office release of him taking topless summers in Siberia – biceps rippling as he casts out fishing lines, pecs glowing as he rides bare-chested on sweating stallions and shoulders straining as he swims (butterfly – naturally – it's the toughest stroke) in icy lakes. You've also got to wonder about his release of an eighty-minute video called *Let's Do Judo with Vladimir Putin*. Also about the occasion he boasted to George W. Bush that his dog Connie was 'bigger and stronger and faster' than Barney, the US president's dog. And finally, it's hard not to worry that just about the only time we've seen Putin smiling in front of a camera was when he allowed that same Labrador to interrupt a press conference with Angela Merkel – knowing full well that the German Chancellor had been terrified of dogs ever since she was bitten as a child.

Such no-willy waving can also be seen in Putin's domestic and foreign policy. Because if there's one thing that makes Putin feel better than riding and swimming, it's annexing and fixing. Dozens of journalists have been assassinated while he's been in the Kremlin. Russian troops have stormed into the Crimea. He has funded and bolstered far-right-wing political parties all over Europe. Russian agents and hackers worked to change the outcome of the last US election and there's more than a whiff of their involvement in the Brexit vote too.

Putin has woven so many complicated webs that it's impossible to know where his influence ends – but perhaps the biggest mystery about this master of secrets and misinformation is that any of his behaviour should have surprised us. And yet, somehow … During the

---

* Putin has actually boasted about being a school bully on his official website.

2012 US presidential campaign, in those happy days when Mitt Romney was the craziest thing the Republican Party could throw at us, the man-who-once-took-a-twelve-hour-road-trip-with-his-dog-strapped-to-the-roof-of-his-station-wagon named Russia as America's 'top geopolitical foe'. Barack Obama joked in return that 'The 1980s are now calling to ask for their foreign policy back, because the Cold War's been over for twenty years.'

But for once, Romney was right. Westerners might have hoped that they had won the Cold War, but Vladimir Putin had never stopped fighting it.

The clues were all there. We might have had some indication from the fact that Putin was an ex-KGB hardman. After all, the KGB was rather better known for spreading fake news and murdering dissidents than it was for its friendly tolerance of liberal democracies. But just in case we didn't spot that glaring indication, and soon after he burned all his files from his East German posting, Putin declared the fall of the Berlin Wall and collapse of Soviet Russia 'the greatest geopolitical catastrophe of the century'. Then, in his first speech after he came to power in Moscow, he made dark threats about anyone who dared to oppose Russia – and he made good on them by invading Chechnya and killing tens of thousands of people.

He also quickly took control of Russian TV channels and started putting out relentless pro-himself and anti-Western propaganda. He had journalists arrested. It was just like the bad old days of Communism – except now, instead of being the enforcing arm of a political party, the secret service – now renamed the FSB – pretty much ran the government.

Another thing that remained constant from the days of the KGB was the way Putin's opponents kept dying in 'mysterious' circumstances. And when I say 'mysterious', I actually mean 'really quite crazily obvious' circumstances. Like when Alexander Litvinenko made the mistake of accusing Putin of running a mafia state and said that he had arranged the execution of journalist Anna Politkovskaya. (She in turn had foolishly accused Putin of arranging the bombing of several apartment buildings in Moscow as a pretext for declaring war on the Chechens – and had been assassinated on the comb-over kleptocrat's birthday.) Litvinenko was killed when two men from Moscow tricked him into drinking tea laced with a rare radioactive poison, polonium-210. A poison that came from a Russian nuclear reactor and left traces all over London, literally showing the assassins' footprints as they moved in on their victim – not to mention the radioactive towel they used to clean their hands afterwards.

Putin's recent attempts to interfere in elections have been just as unsubtle. Banks close to Putin have loaned millions of pounds to French fascist Marine Le Pen. Funny money sloshed around pro-Leave organisations in the UK's Brexit referendum. Several MPs have further accused him of interfering in our 2015 general election.

Then, there's Donald Trump. There are the Russian hacks of the Democratic National Congress and the way they were leaked during election season. There are the funny stories about Trump being filmed taking a golden shower in a Moscow hotel and subsequently blackmailed. There are the less amusing repeated contacts between Trump affiliates and Russian agents during the run-up to the election. There's the fact that Putin sent Donald Trump his congratulations within an hour of Clinton's concession. Putin may now have reason to regret helping out this most wild and unpredictable of allies – but it's worth remembering that when the Russian Duma heard the election result, the gathered assembly broke into applause. It's also worth remembering the way Trump quickly appointed Rex Tillerson as his secretary of state, in spite of the fact that he has billions of dollars of financial interests in Russia and the Kremlin had awarded Tillerson the order of friendship in 2013. Putin's left a trail as glowingly radioactive as the polonium that did for poor old Litvinenko. There's little doubt that vital parts of the current US administration are in Putin's trouser pocket.

Worse still, we all know there's plenty more room in there for other world leaders.

AYN RAND

—

Date of birth/death: *2 February 1905 – 6 March 1982*
In a nutshell: *Evangelist for the virtue of selfishness*
Connected to: *Donald Trump, Rex Tillerson, the Koch brothers, Boris Johnson*

In 1917, when the novelist and political theorist Ayn Rand was twelve years old, she watched as Bolsheviks wrecked her family business in St Petersburg. She didn't like that. In fact, she bore a grudge. She hated Communism so much she decided that only its direct opposite must be true. She proposed an upside-down Marxism. Instead of the workers being the people who produce the things of value in the world, Ayn Rand declared that the bosses and owners and wealthy were the real source of good.

More than that, Rand fed bosses the appealing notion that they deserved their money. In books like *Atlas Shrugged* and *The Fountainhead* she told the rich that they aren't parasites or exploiters or immoral. She celebrated individuals who put themselves first. She portrayed these fortunate souls as superhuman. She urged the rich to keep their money and refuse to help everyone else. In her ultimate counter-intuitive coup, she came up with the theories of the 'virtue of selfishness' and 'enlightened self-interest'. Which are fancy ways of saying: feel free to do whatever the hell you like. Rand backed this up by characterising anyone who wasn't rich as despicable – a 'moocher' class, who deserve contempt instead of help. 'If a man is weak he does not deserve love,' Rand once told an interviewer, with characteristic charm.

I guess you can see where all this is going?

Yes: Ayn Rand is a wanker-magnet. She's tremendously popular with many of our current world leaders. Influential pro-Brexit campaigners Daniel Hannan and Douglas Carswell have produced a book based on Rand's ideas. Boris Johnson has written Rand-inspired articles declaring the rich 'an oppressed minority'. His fellow Tory cabinet minster Sajid Javid claims he once read a scene from *The Fountainhead* when wooing the woman who – remarkably – became his wife. He also told a political film society that the film of the book articulated just 'what I felt'.

US politicians and commentators love Rand even more. Former Federal Reserve chairman Alan Greenspan was a member of Rand's inner circle from the 1950s to the 1980s. The libertarian Rand Paul has declared 'I am a big fan.' Meanwhile, Paul Ryan, Speaker of the House of Representatives and leading Republican climate-change denier, once told an Ayn Rand fanclub: 'The reason I got involved in public service, by and large, if I had to credit one thinker, one person, it would be Ayn Rand.' He also said: 'It's inspired me so much that it's required reading in my office for all my interns and my staff.'

And so it goes on. And on. And on. A bit like her novels. Christopher Hitchens once accurately described these weighty tomes as 'transcendentally awful'. But although the books are unusually bad, they do pull off one clever trick. Rand manages to flatter people like Carswell and Paul Ryan and Rand Paul by telling them that they are the brains and brawn of the world. She tells them they are 'rational' and that they are simply following an unbiased, straightforward truth: 'objectivism'. And the killer blow is that the books are pitched low enough that these not-so-great great thinkers are able to understand them. They are written in basic English, and she keeps the busy plutocrats' attention by leavening her blunt, simple ideas with emotion, sex, guns, explosions and absurd sci-fi-tinged adventure. Even Donald Trump is a fan.

That's right. Donald Trump once claimed to have read a book. And according to Trump, this book – Rand's novel *The Fountainhead* – 'relates to everything'. He especially likes the novel's hero, Howard Roark. Trump has expressed great affinity with this character, who spends 700 pages ranting about everything he doesn't like in the world and then blows things up when he doesn't get his way. Who can say what Trump sees in him?

Elsewhere, Rex Tillerson, Trump's controversial Secretary of State and friend of Vladimir Putin, has said that his favourite book is Rand's biggest novel, *Atlas Shrugged*. *Atlas Shrugged* starts with the famous question 'Who is John Galt?' – and then spends 1,200 long pages explaining.

This book is, as the critic Whittaker Chambers noted, a work of 'shrillness without reprieve'. But it is also compelling. The denouement is particularly mad. It boasts, among other absurd delights, a particle destroyer, a kinky electric torture machine, gratuitous nudity, and a man who introduces himself in the heat of battle and in all earnest as 'Francisco Domingo Carlos Andres Sebastián d'Anconia'. Such bonkers excitement, combined with the high-pitched urgency of Rand's writing and her tempting message that it's okay to be selfish, has appealed to millions of readers over the years. Many of them have gone on to shape our collective destiny.

Talking of destiny, meanwhile, Rand herself lived to the ripe old age of seventy-seven – although in her later years she suffered from lung cancer and set aside her principles so she could claim Medicaid and Social Security. At her funeral in 1982, she had a six-foot floral arrangement in the shape of a dollar sign. Alan Greenspan was there. Five years later, he took over the Federal Reserve. Soon after, the income of the top 1 per cent of households in America began to rise rapidly – while everyone else's slowed.

MILTON FRIEDMAN

—

Date of birth/death: *31 July 1912 – 16 November 2006*
In a nutshell: *Free-market fundamentalist preacher*
Connected to: *Margaret Thatcher, Ronald Reagan, Richard Nixon,*
Henry Kissinger, George W. Bush

According to *The Economist*, Milton Friedman is 'the most influential economist of the second half of the 20th century ... possibly of all of it'.

That's right.

You can blame him.

Before you get too angry, you should also know that Friedman was in some ways an admirable man, as well as an economic genius. His mathematical work at the University of Chicago was brilliant. His papers and books on consumption analysis, the complexity of stabilisation policy and monetary history won him a Nobel Prize. He correctly predicted the stagflation crisis in the 1970s (where high inflation and stagnant demand in national economies blew apart the old post-war consensus). He was also an early defender of gay rights and a forceful critic of the war on drugs.

Okay, he wasn't universally renowned for his good nature or generosity. When he returned journalists' calls, he was notorious for reversing the charges. But he was a gregarious and persuasive speaker, sharp in his observations, consistently amusing and clear, even when discussing the arcana of interest rates. He also had a neat way with aphorisms. He was the man who told the world that 'there is no such thing as a free lunch'.

He also said: 'The only way that has ever been discovered to have a lot of people cooperate together voluntarily is through the free market. And that's why it's so essential to preserving individual freedom.' Which was a curious thing to hear from someone who had lived through World War II and helped in the worldwide non-market determined struggle to defeat the Axis powers.

Just as tellingly, he once declared: 'I'm not in favour of fairness.'

What Friedman was in favour of was markets. He reduced everything to a zero-sum game in which consumers have all the power they need in relation to the suppliers of goods and services, because they are able to shop elsewhere if they don't like what they are getting.

He outlines this idea at the start of the book he and his wife Rose wrote, called *Free to Choose*. There, he talks about the manufacture of pencils, developing on the famous trope that no one person knows how a pencil is made because the various parts like the lead, the rubber and the brass ferule involve a separate series of mining and manufacturing processes too complex and geographically widespread for any one person to master. Friedman contends that there is also a pencil market controlled by a 'price system'.

For pages and pages he delineates the complexities of the manufacture, all the different contributions to the pencil, and the way these can vary – the way forest fires, for instance, can impact the price of wood. He also maintains that consumers are always in control of things at the end-point of the process. If prices go up, they can choose to pay more – or choose to make their pencil last longer, or perhaps buy propelling pencils instead.

It all sounds very smart – but misses the essential thing that any eight-year-old can tell you about the actual end-users of pencils. They don't have any choice. Because they're eight. They're school children. They still have to do the same amount of writing no matter how much the pencil may cost. The truth is that if the price of pencils goes up, most people can't adapt, or look elsewhere. They just suffer …

But Friedman still insists on the primacy of markets, describing them as a kind of perfect system that will correct and control themselves just so long as they are left well enough alone. He doesn't allow for the fact that consumers don't always have a choice. Or that sellers will often cheat those consumers.

Friedman's thinking has led to market structures being imposed in all sorts of ways that they shouldn't. He spread the belief that competition will magically make the education sector more efficient, instead of turning a public service into another place where shareholders get to soak us. He taught that private providers should control our health systems. His followers decided power companies with confusing tariff plans and ever richer owners are somehow better than nationalised utilities. His close personal friends in the George W. Bush administration – like Secretary of Defence Donald Rumsfeld – were even convinced that private security firms like Halliburton should carry out all kinds of security and administrative work in war zones like Iraq. Which worked out just fine …

It's terrifying to go back to the source material and see the specious nature of the writing that has had such influence on our lives. There's plenty more where that pencil theory came from. In *Free to Choose*, Friedman asks in all earnest how it was that Britain managed to expand its economy even more successfully than the USA in the late nineteenth century, given that Britain didn't have comparable land and mineral resources? He answers even more seriously that it's because Britain had a small government and free-market economic policy. He doesn't mention the country's huge coal reserves. Or, even more astonishingly, the fact that it had an empire on which the sun never set. Elsewhere, he just makes things up; especially in his many extrapolations about life in the Soviet Union, for which he can't have had reliable data. But still, millions of people bought the absurd book. It was the non-fiction bestseller in the USA in 1980 and right-wing politicians lapped it up.

And Friedman didn't just comment on economics; he actively prose-lytised. He called himself a 'warrior', determined to eliminate 'government interference in free enterprise, from minimum wage to social welfare programmes'. He loathed nearly all the workings of the state and said that the 'invisible guiding hand' of the free market should 'hold the tiller' instead of any government.

His advocacy bore fruit when the UK Conservative Party was elected to power in 1979. He told the *Washington Post* that Thatcher's election would 'mark the turning away from the welfare state back to the free-market economies of the nineteenth century'. Correctly.

I know all that sounds like a nightmare – unless you like your chimney cleaned by sooty six-year-olds – but Friedman loved the Victorians. He also liked to claim the lack of regulation in the nineteenth- and early-twentieth-century markets did more to improve the life of the common man than at any other time. Incorrectly.

And Friedman was soon jetting off to meet the new prime minister and persuade her to make things more Dickensian. She told him she would be delighted to do just that, so he wrote a *Newsweek* column entitled 'Hooray for Margaret Thatcher'.

Back home in the USA he was also soon serving as a member of President Reagan's Economic Advisory Board. He persuaded Reagan that there was a 'natural rate' of unemployment and that having a few million people out of work was probably a good way to stop stagflation. So Reagan made sure unemployment hit record highs for years.

There was also Chile. Friedman's acolytes from the Chicago School had been there, right alongside the military, in 11 September 1973 when Pinochet overthrew the popular government of Salvador Allende in a bloody coup. Immediately after, the 'Chicago Boys' put into practice the teachings of Friedman's other famous book, *Capitalism and Freedom*. As Pinochet began torturing and killing tens of thousands of his people, the economists started tearing apart Chile's industry, privatising, throwing the markets open, destroying local workers with free trade, overseeing 375 per cent rises in inflation and claiming that the problem was that their economic medicine hadn't been strong enough.

Pinochet was soon getting a bad international reputation for rounding people up and shooting them in football stadiums – but still Friedman himself came down to help in 1975, meeting Pinochet, broadcasting lectures on national TV, asking for his usual formula of deregulation and 'shock treatment'. He wrote in his diaries that Pinochet (although a mass murderer) was worried about the social consequences of rising unemployment. Friedman told him to cut government spending by another 25 per cent. That's right. Where even Pinochet had qualms, Friedman had none. And so millions lost their jobs. The economy didn't recover for almost a decade, when

Pinochet at last changed course. Friedman later falsely claimed that Pinochet's adaptation of free-market policies ameliorated his rule and led to the country's transition to democratic government in 1990 ... After almost twenty years of tyranny and the torture and murder of thousands. But hey! At least the invisible hand of the market determined which brand of cattle prod the police used to electrocute people.

Now you can get angry.

Pinochet is fading into bad memory. Chile is moving on. But many of Friedman's other legacies remain with us. Closer to home, you can still blame Friedman for the privatised electricity companies and their huge bills. Blame him if you've heard a Republican politician talking with loathing of 'big government'. If you've lamented paying so damn much to catch a privatised train service, Friedman's at the heart of it.

On a broader level, his ideas provided ideological cover for massive capital accumulation for multinational corporations during the 1980s to 2000s and the belief that markets should be regulated as little as possible. On Friedman's death in 2006, President George W. Bush said, 'His work demonstrated that free markets are the great engines of economic development.' Two years later those engines started grinding and chucking out black smoke. Friedman had missed the 2008 financial crash his ideas helped bring about – and which proved them so catastrophically wrong. Oh well.

RONALD REAGAN

Date of birth/death: 6 February 1911 – 5 June 2004

In a nutshell: *Man who made it rain while convincing everyone the sun was shining*

Connected to: *Milton Friedman, Margaret Thatcher, George W. Bush, Donald Trump*

Media pundits often talk about the 'Overton Window' when referring to the range of ideas that the public will accept. The theory is that for a political policy to float with the public, it has to fit within certain accepted parameters – also known as the 'window of discourse'. The consensus is that in the UK and USA this window has gradually shifted to the right. Ideas that were once thought cruel and preposterous (such as those relating to charging students for higher education, or scrapping healthcare entitlements) are now thought mainstream. One of Ronald Reagan's biggest legacies lies in the work he did to persuade the world to take this rightward shift. But, just as importantly, he also moved another set of parameters. A set, alas, that doesn't yet have a fancy name. But a set that has also had huge impact. Ronald Reagan shifted the boundaries on the preposterous. We could probably call this phenomenon the 'Trump lift'.

Before Reagan, the idea of a TV-star president seemed entirely laughable to the American public. The idea of Ronald Reagan himself seemed laughable, in fact. Here he was, a man who had first made his name as a second-rate B-movie actor and later as the genial host of brazenly partisan and commercial TV slots for the General Electric Company. He was known to have spent a lot of time testifying against his colleagues during the McCarthy era.* He had gained a certain notoriety for his enthusiastic support for the National Rifle Association and for sending the National Guard in to crush student protests. He did that at the University of California in Berkeley, when he was Governor of the state. A student was killed and Reagan commented: 'If it takes a bloodbath, let's get it over with.' He was also known to take advice from an astrologer called Caroll Righter, known as the 'gregarious Aquarius'.†

If he hadn't won the 1980 presidential election, Reagan would just have been a handsome but strange and malicious historical footnote.

But win it he did – and the real absurdity came after he took over the reins. Astrology had nothing on the voodoo he used to steer the American economy. Reagan's greatest superstition was 'supply-side economics'. It was he who set us up for the fall in 2008 – and destroyed American jobs and industry in the process. Reagan believed in something called the Laffer curve. This was a theory devised by

* And it was also later revealed that he had been secretly passing on names to the FBI.

† Reagan would eventually deny he took advice from astrologers. But as Governor of California in the 1960s he told the press he read Righter's column every morning and he even issued an official proclamation of appreciation to Righter. At the press conference where Reagan claimed 'no policy or decision in my mind has ever been influenced by astrology', a White House spokesman was also forced to admit that Nancy Reagan's interest in astrology had at the very least influenced Ronald's scheduling of speeches and trips.

Arthur Laffer from Milton Friedman's famous economics department at the University of Chicago.* It states counter-intuitively (and as it turned out, counter-factually) that government could increase revenue by decreasing taxes. The idea was that the rich would no longer have to spend their time thinking up tax-dodging ruses and so work more productively and contribute more – and so the lower rate would stimulate so much growth that revenues would just grow.

Reagan duly cut taxes on the rich. But there was no swelling of the public coffers. Instead, the deficit rose from about $900 billion to more than $3 trillion. Which is worth writing with all the digits, just so you can get an idea of the ridiculousness of the numbers involved: from 900,000,000,000 to 3,000,000,000,000. More than three times as much as the deficit Reagan spent his whole time complaining about when he was trying to get elected in the first place.

By 1982 he had also succeeded in raising unemployment to above 10 per cent for the first time since the 1930s. Oh, and by 1987 the average amount of 'leisure time' Americans enjoyed in a week fell to 16.6 hours. (In 1973, they'd enjoyed 26.2 hours.) His presidency also saw the first year since 1895 that America didn't have a trade surplus. But don't worry! Some people got richer. That's right. The people who were already rich. Donald Trump, for instance, built the Trump Tower during Reagan's reign. The rest of the top 2 per cent in the country did okay too and we entered the red braces and embossed business-card era of Wall Street growth – the one that would eventually lead to the subprime crisis and the hot fun of the Lehman Brothers collapse.

Lower down there were all-out assaults on unions, next to no growth in the median real wage, a drop in income per person, a huge increase

* 'Milton Friedman I love,' said Laffer. 'How can you not love Milton Friedman?'

in household debt and an economy that grew at a slower rate over the course of the decade than in any ten-year period in the twentieth century since World War II.

Reagan did at least get some things right. By the end of his presidency, once he had ditched many of his earlier economic ideas, he managed to cut inflation. His relentless military build-up also helped him bring about a thawing in the Cold War and led to the eventual collapse of the Soviet Union. For that, he earned the gratitude of millions around the world.

But if we're going to credit Reagan for helping to end the Cold War, he should also take a good part of the blame for our current travails. Most notably, he helped arm, train and finance the radical Islamic Mujahideen fighters in Afghanistan who would go on to form both the Taliban and Al Qaeda, as well as the model for ISIS. He also ensured America remained unpopular around the world. During his presidency American forces were caught meddling unsuccessfully in the Lebanon. They bombed Libya. They shot down an Iranian passenger jet. They invaded Grenada. There was also a preposterous affair where the Americans covertly sold arms to Iranians in order to fund a group called the Contras who were fighting the government in Nicaragua.

Talking of war, Reagan also launched a domestic front. 'We're taking down the surrender flag that has flown over so many drug efforts; we're running up a battle flag,' he said. But this war on drugs largely turned into a war on poor black Americans – one which Reagan had begun when he stated his opposition to affirmative action, his attacks on civil rights leaders and gutting of initiatives like the Civil Rights Commission. His creation of mandatory minimum sentences for possession and supply of drugs had a disproportionate effect on black communities. His signature policy was to introduce stricter sentencing for crack cocaine than normal cocaine. Why impose greater penalties for crack? Because more poor black people used this form of the drug. It was more economical – people used less to get a more intense high. It ripped through black communities and Reagan came right after it. His programme of incarceration helped ensure that, today, there are more black men in jail (often providing free labour) than were enslaved in 1850 – and more who are denied the vote.

And while all this was going on, soft-speaking and kindly-looking Reagan was somehow able to convince his people it was morning in America and the future would only get better. He also helped ensure that his legacy would be forever burnished by right-wing media channels by eliminating the Fairness Doctrine in 1987. Thanks to Reagan, TV and radio news in America no longer had to present a diversity of viewpoints or to be fair or balanced. So we got unfair and unbalanced right-wing channels. And unreality TV. And all that that brought with it. Reagan may have told us it was morning. But really he was marching us into the night.

MARGARET THATCHER

Date of birth/death: *13 October 1925 – 8 April 2013*
In a nutshell: *The wicked witch of Western capitalism*
Connected to: *Milton Friedman, Ronald Reagan, David Cameron*

According to popular mythology, Margaret Thatcher invented Mr Whippy soft-serve ice cream. The story goes that when she worked for Joe Lyons towards the end of the 1940s, this clever young industrial chemist developed emulsifiers that enabled her employer to pump air into the cream and more easily transport and sell it across the country. It isn't true. Like many of the ideas attributed to Mrs T, this one actually originated in America. Soft-serve has been around since at least the 1930s. But it's easy to see why the image has stuck. It symbolises so much about her. It was a way of giving customers less of the good stuff, at less cost and for more profit, while telling them to like it.

Also, Mr Whippy ice cream is cold. Freezing cold.

But the metaphor breaks down at the final stages. Soft-scoop ice cream remains popular with the punters. It's still a successful recipe. Most of the other things Margaret Thatcher worked on have ended in disaster.

A typical Iron Lady soft-scoop scheme was her Milton Friedman-inspired decision to privatise energy companies like British Gas. The wheeze was that she would allow members of the public to buy a few shares. She thereby suggested that she was letting them take a stake in the industry, rather than just selling them back something they already owned – and which their taxes had already paid for. After a huge advertising campaign and profitable launch, the scheme worked out in typical fashion: the chairman and major shareholders quickly gave themselves huge pay rises, prices steadily increased – and the service got steadily worse. There was a gradual descent into the rip-off* culture we are left with today.

And so it went, through all her major initiatives. There was the sell-off of council housing: initially pleasing those who were able to buy their own homes, eventually a major contributor to the ongoing UK property crisis and also the suffering of the younger generation, largely unable to afford their own homes. There was privatising ICI: causing over 15,000 job losses in the North East. There was the sell off of British water providers: bigger bills, more leaks, ever more sewerage pumped into our rivers.

The pattern is clear. But Thatcher's legacy is as much about the psychological as well as the economic and environmental changes she caused. The lasting scars also come from the way she brutally crushed

---

* 'Ripping off' was a term used by a cross-party investigation into energy companies in the UK in March 2017. A report commissioned by David Cameron had discovered that between 2012 and 2015, customers had been made to pay at least £1.4bn a year in 'excessive prices'.

unions in industrial disputes like the miners' strike. The way she used the police as a political army, sending mounted coppers to smash into peaceful protesters at flashpoints like the notorious Battle of Orgreave. The way she tore the heart out of communities around the UK.

Talking of hearts, meanwhile, she taught us to be mean. She told us: 'There is no such thing as society; there are individual men and women and there are families.' Following this unfriendly precept, she supported notorious dictators like Augusto Pinochet and secretly sold arms to Saddam Hussein (while publicly condemning his gassing of his own people). She also lied and deceived. She claimed to be cutting taxes, but actually increased the tax burden for all but the top-rate of income tax payers – and ensured the UK's wealth gap grew ever larger. Finally, she opened us up to economic adventurism. Madsen Pirie, the chair of one of Thatcher's favourite free-market think tanks, the Adam Smith Institute, once gloated: 'We propose things which people regard as being on the edge of lunacy. The next thing you know, they're on the edge of policy.'

One of the Institute's proposals was the Poll Tax in 1990 – a single flat rate per capita tax on every adult in the UK. Under this system, pensioners in tiny houses suddenly found themselves expected to pay more than rich people in huge houses – and its gross inequalities provoked riots and civil disobedience. Thatcher's reign was soon over.

When she came into office, she had famously said: 'I would just like to remember some words of St Francis of Assisi which I think are really just particularly apt at the moment. "Where there is discord, may we bring harmony. Where there is error, may we bring truth. Where there is doubt, may we bring faith. And where there is despair, may we bring hope."'

She failed us all, on all counts. Which explains why the other big myth that grew up around Mrs Thatcher was that they were going to bury her on Ibiza. Why? Because so many people wanted to dance on her grave.

WILLIAM THE CONQUEROR

—

Date of birth/death: *c. 1028 – 9 September 1087*
In a nutshell: *Thug got lucky*
Connected to: *The Queen, Jesus*

William the Conqueror's reign of terror and murder may have faded into the mists of time, but its legacy lives on. The descendants of the gang of bandits he brought over here still control huge amounts of British land and wealth, while his policies have ensured 950 years of inequality.

William (generally known as William the Bastard during his lifetime) was convinced that he was uniquely favoured by his Christian God – and so had a licence to do pretty much whatever the hell he liked. He was a correspondingly harsh and austere man. Surprisingly, it was once thought that people gathered round and made speeches at his funeral about what a jovial and generous fellow William had been. Less surprisingly, this story turned out to be incorrect. It was based on a mistranslation of an ancient chronicle – and the good-hearted man the people were talking about was actually the Abbot of Verdun.

There's only one other recorded instance of William attempting a joke. This was when he pretended to stab one of his Norman abbots with a great big knife. You can imagine how side-splitting his unwilling comedy partner found that.

All the other evidence points to William being a cold-hearted killer. His nature was best demonstrated in the winter of 1069–70, when William put down rebellions in England's northern counties with genocidal savagery.

'The King stopped at nothing to hunt his enemies,' wrote the chronicler Orderic Vitalis. 'He cut down many people and destroyed homes and land … To his shame, William made no effort to control his fury, punishing the innocent with the guilty. He ordered that crops and herds, tools and food be burned to ashes. More than 100,000 people perished of starvation.'

Charles Dickens also wrote a vivid description of the events in his *Child's History of England*:

> *The streams and rivers were discoloured with blood; the sky was blackened with smoke; the fields were wastes of ashes; the waysides were heaped up with dead … In melancholy songs, and doleful stories, it was still sung and told by cottage fires on winter evenings, a hundred years afterwards, how, in those dreadful days of the Normans, there was not, from the River Humber to the River Tyne, one inhabited village left, nor one cultivated field – how there was nothing but a dismal ruin, where the human creatures and the beasts lay dead together.*

Here we can see the clear origins of modern Tory party policy towards the north of England. There are other lasting legacies of William's rule. We can probably blame him for the average Brit being strangely prejudiced against the French, decent food and learning foreign languages. We can certainly blame him because just 0.3 per cent of the UK population owns more than two-thirds of the land in Britain – and 1 per cent of the population owns more than 70 per cent.

William's very first act after he was crowned on Christmas Day 1066 was to claim that every acre of land belonged to him (strictly speaking if you live in the UK, your house still belongs to the monarch). He then parcelled out this booty to the soldiers who fought with him at Hastings, thus beginning feudalism and a landowning system that has stayed with us ever since. And even aside from all the royals, dukes and earls, people with Norman names like Darcy, Percy and Mandeville are still much wealthier than the general population. According to a 2011 survey they also live an average of three years longer than everyone else. There they are: born to rule over us, just because they're descended from a gang of roving bandits who got lucky in one battle in 1066 when a stray arrow landed in Harold's eye. The game is rigged. And it's William's fault.

MEL GIBSON

Date of birth: *3 January 1956*
In a nutshell: *Hollywood actor caught saying bad things on tape –*
and espousing dodgy history on camera
Connected to: *Jesus*

'The Jews are responsible for all the wars in the world. Are you a Jew? What do you think you're looking at, sugar tits?'

So said Mel Gibson on the night of his arrest for drunk-driving in 2006. He has a bad habit of getting caught on tape. In 2010, he was also recorded in conversation with his ex-girlfriend Oksana Grigorieva:

'You go out in public and it's a fucking embarrassment to me. You look like a fucking bitch in heat, and if you get raped by a pack of niggers it'll be your fault. All right? Because you provoked it. You are provocatively dressed all the time, with your fake boobs, you feel you have to show off in tight outfits and tight pants (garbled) you can see your pussy from behind ...'

Later he was arrested for a misdemeanour battery on Oksana.

The staunchly Catholic actor and director's long struggle with alcoholism and related mental-health issues might explain some of this behaviour – but Gibson has also been a malign influence when he's sober. Here in the UK we can lay many of our problems directly at his feet. By his own admission, his 1995 film *Braveheart* has been one of the root causes of the populism that has swamped our island in recent years. 'It certainly woke something up there in Scotland,' said Gibson in a 2017 Press Association interview. And what it woke was anti-English nationalism.

The film is loosely based on the story of William Wallace, a thirteenth- to fourteenth-century aristocrat and briefly the leader of a war against King Edward I of England. 'Loose' in the sense of eight pints of lager and a hot balti working their way through your guts. Gibson (who also directed the film) smeared his face in woad, kilted up in clan tartan and portrayed Wallace as a principled and dedicated patriotic warrior, fond of bellowing lustily as he charges fearlessly into battle. This Wallace is also handy with slogans: 'We can have what we never had before – a country of our own,' he yells. No matter that Scotland had been independent for centuries when the real William Wallace led his murderous campaigns – and would remain so. No matter either that kilts were invented (in England) in the eighteenth century.* No matter that no one had put woad on their face for a good thousand years by the time Wallace was leading his murderous rampages.

---

* The 'traditional' kilt was introduced to Scotland by an Englishman called Thomas Rawlinson in the eighteenth century. Rawlinson, had noticed that the authentic Highland dress worn by his employees north of the border was 'a cumbrous unwieldy habit' so he got the tailor from the local (English) army regiment to design something more suitable. The tailor came up with the kilt design and the rest is history – but maybe not history as Scottish nationalist kilt wearers would have it.

On the subject of those campaigns, Mel Gibson himself acknowledged in a 2009 interview that the real Wallace was probably a 'monster', forever smelling of smoke because he was so fond of burning villages. Mel also – not unreasonably – said that he isn't worried that his character was nothing like the real Wallace and that he may have 'messed up' the history. He was providing a cinematic experience, after all. But then, in the same interview he did go on to say 'Films are there first to entertain, then teach, then inspire.'

So what was *Braveheart* teaching? What did it inspire? If you saw the long queues outside the cinemas in Scotland, and watched as grown men emerged after the film weeping, you'd get a fair idea. Also indicative was the fact that Scottish Nationalist Party activists were ready to greet the tearful crowds with leaflets bearing Gibson's face and slogans like 'independence isn't just history', 'independence, we need it now more than ever' and 'today, it's not just bravehearts who choose independence'. The SNP party leader at the time, Alex Salmond, also joked to a sword-wielding, kilt-wearing crowd at the annual Wallace rally that he would remove the head of the Scottish Secretary Michael Forsyth during the intermission at the film's premiere.

In the years since that recruitment drive, the SNP have been careful to give a veneer of respectability to their separatism, claiming that their brand of nationalism is more inclusive and less xenophobic than all the other nationalisms around the world. They imply without noticeable irony that they are better, because they are Scottish.

In spite of such rationalisations, *Braveheart* still opened the stopper on a poison that has leached into every aspect of British life. It set a tone with its outrageous distortions of reality tied to sentimental flag-waving and outright racism. It helped inspire a resurgence in SNP fortunes and so brought us the misery of the 2014 Scottish Independence Referendum. There it was shown that millions of votes could be won thanks to transparently nonsensical promises about the bonanza that would come from future oil wealth and angry talk about traitors and quislings. That in turn inspired the Leave campaign's combination of foreigner-bashing and lying promises about giving money to the NHS. Not to mention the fact that by defining themselves against the English, the Scottish Nationalists made the English think about themselves as a separate entity too.

'I like to stay out of the politics of other people's nations so I won't go further,' said Mel back in 2009. Which is fine. Having massively distorted history, and helped contribute to decades of ill-feeling, he's decided not to interfere. Let's try not to imagine the mess he'd make if he did ...

RICHARD NIXON

—

Date of birth/death: *9 January 1913 – 22 April 1994*
In a nutshell: *US president caught saying bad things on tape –*
and doing worse all over the world
Connected to: *Donald Trump, Milton Friedman, Henry Kissinger, Chairman Mao*

For millions of people, watching Donald Trump's inauguration on 20 January 2017 felt uniquely horrifying. We had never seen such a malevolent, angry, spiritual mess on that podium before. We had never seen so few people on the Washington mall, such a heavy police presence and so many counter-inaugural protests and riots. It felt like something new and frightening.

But it's the doom of every generation to feel like they're creating history afresh. Our experience wasn't so unique. When Republican Richard Milhous Nixon growled out the oath of office in January 1969, there were plenty of people who were just as upset. The famous gonzo journalist Hunter S. Thompson described the event as 'a king-hell bummer'. There were violent counter-inaugural demonstrations, there was fear and there was loathing. Nixon's address to the nation was better received than Trump's, after he promised to strive for unity and to turn 'swords into ploughshares' – but the event still presaged doom to many. Writing a month after the inauguration Thompson predicted that by 1972 there would be 'violent revolution' or some kind of 'shattering upheaval'. As it turned out, he was wrong. But only by a matter of two years.

Nixon today is best known for Watergate, the scandal that brought down his presidency in August 1974. It started off as a small thing – a strange story about a break-in to Democratic National Committee headquarters at the Watergate office complex in Washington, DC. The burglars were found to have a curious amount of cash on them when they were apprehended, and Carl Bernstein and Bob Woodward, two junior reporters from the *Washington Post*, followed that money back to the US president. Nixon had been trying to steal information about his political rivals.

And that wasn't all. During the course of the investigation it emerged that Nixon had also been secretly taping the White House itself, and his own conversations. Among his sweary tirades came revelations that the original Watergate burglars were being paid hush-money, references to blackmail payments, insults about the American people and shocking revelations about Nixon's character. 'He is humorless to the point of being inhumane. He is devious,' said the *Chicago Tribune*, up until then a paper that had supported Nixon. 'He is vacillating. He is profane. He is willing to be led. He displays dismaying gaps in knowledge. He is suspicious of his staff. His loyalty is minimal.' Ouch.

Watergate was a shocking crime, a landmark in twentieth-century journalism and it ensured that every revelation of a political outrage ever since has had the suffix -gate attached to it. But it wasn't the worst thing Nixon did.

His life and career was one long assault on decency. One of his most enduring legacies was his ingenious development of negative campaigning techniques. He launched hundreds of attacks on political opponents, hired men to spread false rumours, put out fake press releases to trick newspapers and unsuspecting members of the electorate. Fake news, in other words. And Nixon didn't only pioneer the spreading of political misinformation – he proved that it worked, in election after election.

Possibly the dirtiest trick he pulled was to delay the end of the Vietnam War in order to undermine Hubert Humphrey, his rival in the 1968 presidential race. Humphrey was the current vice president in an administration whose polling was steadily getting better. If President Lyndon Johnson had been able to end the murderous war in time for the election … Well …

Johnson almost did it too. He had a deal in the works with Russia and the North and South Vietnamese – but a man called Henry Kissinger who had insider information alerted Nixon. Nixon told his aide Harry Robbins Haldeman to 'monkey wrench' the peace initiative. He got Republican party operatives to convince the South Vietnamese president to stall the talks (with the promise of a better deal for him if a Republican administration got in). Nixon also told his vice-presidential pick Spiro Agnew to threaten the CIA director that he could lose his job if he didn't help out. The peace deal fell through. Nixon won the election. The war ground on with the loss of thousands more lives.

And once Nixon got in power, according to Bob Woodward, he used the office of president as an implement of personal revenge. He spent his time trying to get even with people – and bombing the crap out of Vietnam.

Early in 1972, after dropping millions of tonnes of munitions on Vietnam and its neighbours, Nixon sent a memo to Kissinger (who was by then his National Security Advisor), saying he knew the campaign had achieved nothing: 'K. We have had 10 years of total control of the air in Laos and V.Nam. The result = Zilch.'

This zilch memo was sent on 3 January. The day before Nixon had appeared on CBS saying the campaign had been 'very, very effective'. He knew there were polls saying people approved of the bombing and taking a tough line. And there was another election on the horizon. So he kept at it. He even ordered more intense attacks. And it worked. Politically. Fresh polls showed that the bombing of Vietnam remained popular. 'It's two to one for bombing,' Kissinger said, triumphantly. In that year, the US dropped 1.1 million tonnes of bombs with the ruination and loss of thousands and thousands of lives and no military gain. No matter. Kissinger remarked in October that one particularly intense raid on 8 May had 'won the election' for Nixon.

But of course, just twenty days after that brutal raid, the botched Watergate break-in occurred. Within a couple of years, Nixon was fighting for his political life, attacking the press, doing his utmost to undermine the judiciary who were holding him to account, and lying and lying about it all to his electorate. 'People have got to know whether or not their president is a crook,' he said during a televised Q&A in November 1973. 'Well, I'm not a crook. I've earned everything I've got.'

Alexander P. Butterfield, deputy to H. R. Haldeman and the man who revealed the existence of Nixon's secret tapes, didn't agree. 'The whole thing was a cesspool,' he said years later. The public saw it that way too. By August 1974, Nixon saw the writing on the wall and resigned. He spent the next twenty years before his death in 1994 maintaining that he hadn't done anything so very wrong.

Hunter S. Thompson wrote his obituary for *Rolling Stone* magazine. First line: 'He was a crook.' Unfortunately, Thompson didn't survive to see Nixon's spiritual successor Donald Trump take office. Nor to lament the fact that Nixon had predicted and endorsed Trump's candidacy back in 1988, after the then real-estate magnate appeared on a TV show. 'I did not see the program,' wrote the disgraced president, 'but Mrs Nixon told me that you were great … As you can imagine, she is an expert on politics and she predicts that whenever you decide to run for office, you will be a winner!'

Thanks, Nixon.

Other scandals ending in -Gate

- Nipplegate – relating to a 'wardrobe malfunction' that exposed one of Janet Jackson's breasts during the half-time show of the 2004 Super Bowl.
- Betsygate – allegations that leading pro-Brexit Conservative MP Iain Duncan Smith put his wife Betsy on his payroll without her doing any work.
- Camillagate – the release of a taped conversation in which Prince Charles said he'd like to live inside Camilla's trousers. Maybe as a Tampax.
- Monicagate – named after Bill Clinton's relations with his intern Monica Lewinsky.
- Piggate – the allegation that David Cameron put his penis where he ought not to have put his penis at a dinner party where whole pig heads were served.
- Pussygate – taped conversations with Donald Trump declaring he'd like to kiss a woman and that 'when you're a star, they let you do it. You can do anything … grab them by the pussy.'
- And, best of all: Gategate – the allegation that Tory minister Andrew Mitchell called a policeman a pleb when asked to use a different gate to leave Downing Street on his bicycle.

CHAIRMAN MAO

—

Date of birth/death: *26 December 1893 – 9 September 1976*
In a nutshell: *Killed millions of people for the sake of communism – but actually*
helped usher in an age of ultra-capitalism
Connected to: *Henry Kissinger, Richard Nixon*

Just like Milton Friedman and Ayn Rand, Mao Zedong had big economic theories and he was determined to put them into action. Just like Rand and Friedman, he would claim he had reached his ideas through 'objective analysis'. Just like Rand and Friedman, he made life miserable for millions.

But unlike his two capitalist mirror images, Mao believed in central planning rather than market forces. Unlike Friedman and Rand, he also didn't just leave the work to acolytes. Mao got his hands dirty.

When he got to power in 1949, Mao had already had a good twenty years of fighting for Communism. He'd been hard at it since the late 1920s and – to the immense misfortune of everyone around him – had had an awful lot of luck.

Probably his biggest break came in the Long March of 1934–35 where Mao beat the odds (partly thanks to his willingness to abandon children, the sick and the elderly) to hurry 100,000 people away from encircling nationalist forces.* But even after that, his ascent wasn't a foregone conclusion. If the Japanese had not invaded mainland China in 1937, things might have been very different. They simultaneously distracted the Nationalist government, while forcing more and more people into the Communists' arms with their acts of brutal repression. After the Nanking massacre, for instance, the Red Army grew from 50,000 to 500,000 strong. And it kept on growing until Mao's last enemies surrendered in 1949.

By this time Mao had already caused thousands of deaths. At the Siege of Changchun alone, his forces killed as many people as the bomb on Hiroshima. 'Peaceful methods can not suffice,' he said – and he stood by this principle for the rest of his life. He also stood by his private swimming pool. He was said to most enjoy dictating policy from beside the water. When he wasn't in bed, anyway. Yet while Mao was renowned for being personally lazy, he also got an awful lot done.

One of the chubby chairman's big theories was that China should change from an agricultural to an industrial economy – farming should be collectivised, and targets set for grain production and distribution. He called this the Great Leap Forward and began to put it into practice in 1957. By 1958, he was telling his inner circle that: 'Working like this, with all these projects, half of China may well have to die. If not half, one-third, or one-tenth – 50 million – die.'

It turns out that last figure wasn't a bad estimate. Scholars now say that the famines caused by the Great Leap Forward, the requisition

---

* Mao made sure he didn't tire himself on the march too much. He was carried lots of the way on a litter, filling in the time reading books.

of grain based on falsified figures for harvests, and related droughts and flooding killed between 15 and 45 million people.

Following this disaster, Mao lost some of his grip on power. Members of the Communist Party began liberalising the economy and undoing his Marxist reforms – although Mao kept his grip on the army and the ruthless secret police force he'd been building up over the past decade or so. He began to mobilise again. Demonstrating a fondness for the word 'great' that would be unmatched until Donald Trump came to power, he next instituted the Great Proletarian Cultural Revolution of 1966.

Predictably enough, 'great' turned out to be a serious misnomer. The Cultural Revolution was unremittingly awful. The basic premise here was that there was too much of an elite in China, that the people should be placed in direct control of everything, and that Mao and his newly fanaticised followers in the Red Guard were really, really sick of experts. Thousands of schools and universities across China were closed. Intellectuals were forced out of the cities to be 're-educated' by peasants in the countryside. More millions were killed. Oh well, said Mao, 'China is such a populous nation, it is not as if we cannot do without a few people.'

During the Cultural Revolution Mao also made sure that his extreme vision of Marxism–Leninism was put back into practice. Private enterprises were nationalised, and private property was taken under state control. But such reforms didn't last much beyond his death in 1976. His successors quickly began dismantling them and opening China up for trade and market reform. The thing they didn't dismantle was Mao's one-party state and its powerful system of repression: the giant army, the ruthless police and subservient media. Ironically enough, these were the very things that enabled the Chinese government to push through rapid capitalistic reforms in the 1980s, crush the resistance to them at Tiananmen Square and then go on to set up rigorously policed enterprise parks all over the country. If it wasn't for Mao's state apparatus, China wouldn't have been able to build and maintain the low-tax, low-regulation, high-security and maximum-secrecy fenced-off zones where cowed and subservient workers manufacture so many cheap consumer goods.

So it is that Mao's most enduring legacy lies in feeding the global capitalist machine he despised. We have him to thank for our smart-phones. But also for the fact that so many Western countries have become post-industrial wastelands. Places with low job security and frightened voters looking to demagogic leaders like Donald Trump who promise to bring them jobs again. Actually, come to think of it, maybe Mao will help bring down capitalism after all …

In 1973, Nixon's Secretary of State Henry Kissinger visited Chairman Mao. Mao had a lot of problems on his mind, chief among them, women.

'Let them go to your place,' he said to Kissinger. 'They will create disasters. That way you can lessen our burdens … Do you want our Chinese women? We can give you 10 million.'

Dr Kissinger laughed that Mao was 'improving his offer'.

Mao went on: 'By doing so we can let them flood your country with disaster and therefore impair your interests. In our country we have too many women, and they have a way of doing things. They give birth to children and our children are too many.'

'It is such a novel proposition,' said Kissinger. 'We will have to study it.'

The leaders next spoke briefly about the threat of nuclear apocalypse posed by the Soviet Union, but Mao was soon back with bigger concerns:

'We have so many women in our country that don't know how to fight.'

At this point, US State Department papers show that the Assistant Chinese Foreign Minister, Wang Haijung, cautioned Mao that the public might get annoyed if they found out what he had been saying. Kissinger and Mao agreed to strike the words from the record. They were only made public in 2008.

HENRY KISSINGER

—

Date of birth: *27 May 1923*

In a nutshell: *The shadow behind most of the evil thrones in the last fifty years*

Connected to: *Everyone*

'Why do they hate us?' ask the pundits on American right-wing TV and talk radio. They generally quickly answer that it's because they are 'jealous of our freedoms and lifestyle'. Poor benighted foreigners see hamburgers, Ford Mustangs and Miley Cyrus videos and can't help but go foaming crazy in frustration and rage. You would too if all you had were sand, mullahs and posters of your Dear Leader.

But there's a simpler explanation for all the anti-American feeling in the world: Henry Kissinger. People hate the USA because of Henry Kissinger, the things he did, the things he made other people do and the long shadow he has cast ever since serving as Secretary of State under Presidents Nixon and Ford in the 1970s.

That may sound like exaggeration – but it's actually a challenge to overstate Kissinger's influence. If there's anything in the world that's currently scaring, annoying or killing people, chances are that Kissinger's somewhere in the mix. He was the one who first encouraged Pakistan to use radical Islam to destabilise Soviet-leaning forces in Afghanistan, and so unleash a worldwide wave of jihad. It was his diplomacy that helped ensure the USA would become reliant on Saudi oil. He made sure that the USA started to sell serious military hardware to the sheikhs. He helped lock in Israel's veto over US policy in the Middle East. He made sure the US abandoned its Kurdish allies to Saddam Hussein in Iraq. Kissinger armed and propped up the Shah of Iran, trained his notorious secret police, and paved the way for the 1979 Islamic revolution. He first encouraged China to open up to market capitalism. He even caused trouble in Syria that would come home to roost decades later when he infuriated Hafez al-Assad by encouraging Egypt to sign a separate peace deal with Israel to one he'd told Assad he'd been working on. Assad told Kissinger that his actions would 'release demons hidden under the surface of the Arab world'. Which turned out to be putting it mildly.

It's also hard to overstate the brutal nature of the realpolitik he pursued. One of his most notorious war crimes was to conspire with Nixon to prolong the Vietnam War for five pointless and bloody years in order to help Tricky Dicky win the White House. As the war went on, Kissinger oversaw the bombing of both Cambodia and Laos, directly causing (by his own estimation) around 50,000 deaths and ushering the nightmare rule of the Khmer Rouge* in the process.

---

* In 1975, Kissinger asked the Thai foreign minister how many people the Khmer Rouge had killed and said: 'Tens of thousands? You should tell the Cambodians that we will be friends with them. They are murderous thugs, but we won't let that stand in the way. We are prepared to improve relations with them. Tell them the latter part, but don't tell them what I said before.'

In 1973, after he signed a peace treaty whose terms were almost exactly the same as the one he helped scupper in 1968, he was awarded a Nobel Peace Prize.

'I deeply cherish this honour,' said Kissinger.

'Political satire has become obsolete,' said the comedian Tom Lehrer.

1973 was a bumper year for Kissinger. While he was winning the Nobel Peace Prize, he was also ensuring General Pinochet deposed Salvador Allende, the President of Chile, in a brutal coup. Soon Pinochet's junta, many of them now paid contacts of the CIA and US military, were murdering opponents in football stadiums, wrecking the economy and wiping out democratic resistance. Kissinger liked this situation so much he pulled a similar trick in Argentina, helping to make sure Isabel Perón was deposed and that the military were quickly engaged in the disappearance of thousands of dissidents and innocents there too.

By this time, Kissinger was also getting involved in Indonesia. When he was visiting the country with President Ford, Indonesia's corrupt military dictator Suharto told Kissinger he was planning to invade East Timor. Kissinger told Suharto he wouldn't object so long as it was done 'fast' – and that the invasion should be delayed until he got back to Washington. Suharto waited for one day. The following war lasted six years between 1975 and 1981. It's been estimated that a quarter of the local population died.

But Kissinger was used to a high death toll. As well as the slaughter in Vietnam, he'd also supported Pakistan in the genocide it carried out in Bangladesh during the 1971 war of independence. As the bodies piled up, the US Consul General in Dhaka Archer Blood sent a telegram to Washington accusing the government of 'moral bankruptcy'. Kissinger called him a 'maniac' and had him fired. Once the war was over, and at least half a million people had died, Kissinger commented, 'No one can bleed anymore about the dying Bengalis.'

He continued to charm the world in similar style long after he left the government. Following the massacre at Tiananmen Square in 1989 he accused demonstrators of provoking the Chinese government into 'rash acts' by occupying the main square of its capital city. He also commented chillingly on the million-murdering Mao that if China remained united, many of its citizens would come to think of him in the same way as they do the emperor Qin Shihuang, 'whose excesses were later acknowledged by some as a necessary evil'.

And Kissinger continued to be involved in foreign policy, advising leaders around the world for considerable personal gain. He supported the invasion of Iraq and frequently lent his counsel to George W. Bush. But he was less keen on taking part in the 9/11 Commission, because to do so he would have had to reveal how much the Saudi royal family paid him for his opinions.

Deep into his nineties, he continued to advise Hillary Clinton and Obama about their drone-led foreign policy.* He had less to say about a tape from the Nixon White House that emerged in 2010 in which he was heard telling Nixon not to help Jews escape oppression in the Soviet Union because it was 'not an objective of American foreign policy'. Kissinger himself had escaped Nazi Germany in 1938. But he'd still said to his boss: 'If they put Jews into gas chambers in the Soviet Union it is not an American concern. Maybe a humanitarian concern.' Maybe. And it's maybe that kind of attitude that has done so much to stain America's reputation around the world.

---

* And incidentally contributing to the scuppering of Clinton's election chances when she outraged Bernie Sanders supporters by calling Kissinger her 'friend', saying he was someone who would continue to help her shape her foreign policy should she win the election.

SPECIAL FRIEND of RUSSIA

REX TILLERSON

Date of birth: *23 March 1952*

In a nutshell: *Blatant Putin stooge*

Connected to: *Vladimir Putin, Donald Trump, the Koch brothers, Henry Kissinger*

When Donald Trump appointed Rex Tillerson as his Secretary of State, most people in the world didn't know much about this newly powerful and influential man. But that doesn't mean that he hadn't been working tirelessly to make the world more polluted, dangerous and corrupt.

By the time he took up his appointment in early 2017, Tillerson had spent forty years cheerfully working for Exxon, one of the world's chief producers of greenhouse gases. In 2006, Tillerson became the chief executive of the oil giant (by then called ExxonMobil), and although he reversed a long-held company policy of denying the dangers of man-made climate change, he did little to improve its record of spreading confusion and noxious gases.

Plenty of the latter came from his mouth. At a shareholder meeting in 2013, he said:

'Notwithstanding all the advancements that have been made in gathering more data, instrumenting the planet so that we understand how climate conditions on the planet are changing, notwithstanding all that data, our ability to project with any degree of certainty the future is continuing to be very limited.'

So that's clear. At the same meeting Tillerson claimed that the 'temperature record of the last decade' has been 'relatively flat' – which it hadn't.

But more than Tillerson's words it's ExxonMobil's actions under his leadership that raised the temperature. They continued to fund politicians and organisations* that work to stop action on climate change. They also continued to develop the tar sands extraction technique although it is among the most carbon-heavy of fuel sources.

Nor did Exxon slow down on their drilling work around the world. Plenty would argue that it's bad enough that Tillerson has overseen these international efforts to make sure that fossil fuels aren't left in the ground, where they do no harm. But Tillerson has become especially controversial because it's also turned out he has close ties to Vladimir Putin's Russian regime. He has previously been the director of a joint US and Russian oil company called Exxon Neftegas. He has made multi-million-dollar business deals with Putin. He has become a buddy with Putin's frightening head of security Igor Sechin. They've all been getting on so well that in 2013 the Russian state even gave Tillerson the Order of Friendship medal for his services to developing

---

* Like the American Legislative Exchange Council. Even BP, Shell and Google said this group was too obstructionist and stopped funding it. (It has also been funded by the Koch brothers.)

cooperation in the energy sector. And in 2014, Tillerson called for sanctions not to be applied to Russia when it came under international pressure thanks to Putin's aggression in Ukraine. Tillerson, according to John Hamre, the CEO of the Center for Strategic and International Studies (on whose board Tillerson sits), 'has had more interactive time with Vladimir Putin than probably any other American, with the exception of Dr Henry Kissinger'.

That's right. Of course, Kissinger has been cosying up to Putin for years. He's also been urging Trump to make deals with Putin – and busily dismissing worries about Tillerson's close relationship to Putin. 'I pay no attention to the argument that he is too friendly to Russia,' Kissinger told a non-profit pro-China organisation in December 2016. 'As head of Exxon it's his job to get along with Russia. He would be useless as the head of Exxon if he did not have a working relationship with Russia.'

Talking of 'useless', Tillerson's early days as Secretary of State were chaotic even by the standards of Trump's regime. As well as having to field a lot of awkward questions about his links to Russia, Tillerson also almost accidentally started World War III when he suggested that the USA might block access to man-made islands in the South China Sea, prompting Chinese state media to warn of 'large-scale' repercussions.

Tillerson caused more eyebrow lifting when he went against decades of protocol and refused to take the press corps with him when he went on his first diplomatic tour to Asia. He told the press he intended to avoid them until he had a specific message to deliver. But he did take a journalist with him from a hitherto little-known outlet called the *Independent Journal Review*. This reporter later said he tried to ask Tillerson about Putin, but the Secretary of State was so cagey that his answer 'wasn't even worthy of inclusion'. But there was one fascinating revelation in the interview. Tillerson claimed he hadn't wanted the job of Secretary of State and wouldn't have taken it if his wife Renda St Clair hadn't told him to. He said that after Trump offered him the position he went to his Texas home where Renda shook her finger in his face and said: 'I told you God's not through with you.' Chances are that someone even more powerful probably isn't through with Tillerson either: Vladimir Putin will be watching his friend and business partner very carefully.

THE KOCH BROTHERS

—

Date of birth: *David Koch – 3 May 1940; Charles Koch – 1 November 1935*
In a nutshell: *It's pronounced like coke, but they're still cocks*
Connected to: *Donald Trump, Rex Tillerson, George W. Bush*

'The biggest company you've never heard of,' according to David Koch is the huge oil, gas, chemical and paper conglomerate he controls with his brother Charles. But even if you don't know about Koch Industries, chances are you've felt its effects.

If you live in America you've probably used one of the products manufactured by the company, which makes everything from cups, to carpets, to plastics, to fuel. And if you don't, well, you've breathed the air they've helped to dirty.*

---

* A study from the University of Massachusetts at Amherst's Political Economy Research Institute named Koch Industries one of the top ten air polluters in the United States.

It is, in other words, a major contributor to global warming. Not that the Koch brothers would say that this is a problem. In fact, they'd go out of their way to deny the problem exists. Or, better still, to get someone else to deny it for them.

David Koch himself once told *New York* magazine that he wouldn't even be worried if global warming were real, because the heating of the planet would result in longer growing seasons in the Northern Hemisphere, allowing the Earth to 'support more people' because it could produce more food.

Put that way, global warming sounds pretty great. Who needs polar bears anyway? No wonder David and his brother have spent so many millions of dollars trying to stop people worrying about it. The fact that their companies directly profit from burning fossil fuels probably has nothing to do with their eagerness to set up think tanks and fund lobby groups. Nor with their habit of giving great big piles of money to people willing to forward their agenda.

Some of these latter have been controversial. It's well known that at least 97 per cent of environmental scientists believe humans contribute to global warming. What's less well known is what the other 3 per cent think – and why. But we got a partial explanation in 2015 when Greenpeace released a revealing sheaf of documents.

These related to an academic from the Harvard-Smithsonian Center for Astrophysics called Willie Soon. He had spent years vociferously putting forward the theory that global warming is caused by solar variation rather than human activity – and that anyway, the twentieth century really wasn't that hot compared with other time periods. Soon had come under a lot of criticism from scientists who didn't like his methodology, but had also been widely cited in the media and by Republican politicians eager to refute mainstream climate science, making him something of a figurehead for climate-change deniers.

The documents Greenpeace released showed that although Soon had been singularly unlucky at getting funding from the usual bodies that fund academic research, he had been paid huge amounts by oil companies like Exxon, and also through bodies funded by Charles Koch and his brother David. He took $230,000 from the Charles G. Koch Foundation for instance, and another $324,000 through a trust used by the Koch brothers. He was also awarded a medal of courage by the George C. Marshall Institute, which was partially funded by – wait for it – the Koch brothers.

The full title of this splendid honour was the 'Courage in Defense of Science Award'. When he received the award a 'humbled and honoured' Willie Soon said: 'Science and its practice are no longer free and willing today but instead are constantly terrorized by research funding gravy trains and group thinking.' Presumably he'd rather an oil pipeline than a gravy train.

Elsewhere, the brothers have set up dozens of variously mysterious and impressive-sounding organisations like the Heritage Foundation, which argue that 'scientific facts' don't support the notion of 'catastrophic' anthropogenic global warming. According to *USA Today*, another one of these groups, Americans for Prosperity, spent $20 million in federal lobbying in 2008 while the Obama administration was working to reduce greenhouse gas emissions. In Senate filings, company officials said they would lobby to 'oppose restraints on production and use of energy'. The bill the administration was working on never became law.

The brothers didn't just oppose Obama's environmental legislation. They are also hardcore libertarians, influenced by the usual mix of Ayn Rand and Milton Friedman seasoned with an extra dash of Margaret Thatcher's other favourite 'thinker', Friedrich Hayek. Hayek was convinced that government control of decision-making leads to tyranny. To rescue us from such peril, the Koch brothers set about making sure the government couldn't work as it wanted. Most notoriously, Americans for Prosperity funded many of the distinctly astroturfy 'grassroots' organisations that turned into the Tea Party, as well as training activists and giving people talking points (nay, yelling points) for town hall meetings and interactions with politicians … And when the Tea Party started getting people into the House of Representatives, the brothers maintained a direct line to many of them. They became so influential that when the Speaker of the House John Boehner needed votes to prevent a government shutdown in 2011, he appealed directly to David Koch.

Since then, the brothers have gone from strength to strength and pumped more millions into campaigning. David attended Trump's victory-night party and was soon jetting down to Palm Beach for private meetings with the new president. At the same time, the liberal Center for American Progress reported that a third of Trump's transition team had ties to the Kochs. Vice President Pence, meanwhile, received hundreds of thousands of dollars in campaign contributions from the Kochs when he was governor of Indiana, and spoke at Americans for Prosperity shindigs. When Pence was picked for VP, Trump's counsellor Kellyanne Conway* said: 'Much like Koch Industries, Mike Pence picks the right fights.' Presumably he's going to start kicking the crap out of polar bears soon then.

---

* Just in case you were wondering, Conway (the woman who gave the world the expression 'alternative facts' when talking about the lies the White House was spreading about the size of Trump's inauguration crowd) used to be in the pay of – you guessed it – Americans for Prosperity. She also took money from the Koch-funded 'Independent Women's Forum'. And yes, that is taking the word 'independent' to its absolute limits. Expect plenty of similar stretchers in the not too distant future. Expect also to hear plenty more about those in the company of the Koch brothers – and to breathe ever dirtier air.

THOMAS MIDGLEY JR

‒

Date of birth/death: *18 May 1899 – 2 November 1944*
In a nutshell: *Man with an unusual talent for inventing trouble*
Connected to: *Henry Ford*

In 1921 Thomas Midgley solved a significant issue for the early automobile industry. Back then, the fuel in engines would often burn too quickly, causing temporary losses in power. This caused a loud pinging sound known as engine knocking. Midgley discovered that if you added lead to petrol* the problem went away.

Alas, there was a drawback. Lead is poisonous. It can cause heart attacks. It is also a neurotoxin. It can seriously damage the brain and nervous system. It can cause blindness, deafness, insomnia, cancer, kidney failure, fits and convulsions. In sufficient quantities it can cause terrifying hallucinations – and still more terrifying comas and death.

---

* Specifically, a compound called tetraethyllead.

And I know I'm not telling you anything new in spelling out the danger of lead. If I'd said the same things in 1921, no one would have been surprised either. Its dangers were well known. That's why when three giant corporations, General Motors, Standard Oil of New Jersey and Du Pont, took Midgley's new fuel to market they didn't call the special additive 'lead', they called it 'Ethyl' anti-knock compound. It was a storming success. Midgley was feted the world over. He won a medal from the American Chemical Society. His fuel powered cars around the world. And killed people.

Midgley had personal experience of the dangers of his invention. In 1923, he had to take a long break in Florida to recover from the effects of lead poisoning. 'After about a year's work in organic lead,' he wrote in January, 'I find that my lungs have been affected and that it is necessary to drop all work and get a large supply of fresh air.'

But that didn't stop him advocating for Ethyl. Over the next year and a half more than a dozen people would drop dead at the plants producing the new petrol, and several more lost their minds. 'These men probably went insane because they worked too hard,' said a spokesman. But the press remained irritatingly curious. One particularly nasty run of hallucinating workers, culminating in five deaths, caused so much unwanted publicity that Midgley called a press conference. In front of the gathered journalists, he poured Ethyl over his hands. He also took a long theatrical sniff of it, and declared he could do the same every day without harm. Soon afterwards he was once again diagnosed with lead poisoning.

Midgley moved on to other projects. But the lead remained in our cars. At the worst point, in the USA alone, 5,000 people a year died from lead-related heart disease. An estimated 68 million children received dangerous exposures.

But poisoning more than half the world was not Midgley's most enduring legacy. Lead petrol was mainly phased out by the 1980s, meaning its ill effects were only really felt by older generations.* We're still dealing with the after-effects of one of his other brainwaves.

In the 1920s, the motors in refrigerators relied on dangerous – and frequently flammable – gases. When asked to provide a solution, Midgley took just three days to come up with an apparently harmless alternative called Freon. This was a non-corrosive, non-flammable and safely breathable compound. Full name: dichlorodifluoromethane. It was the world's first CFC. And it was incredibly successful. Soon it was in fridges everywhere, not to mention aerosols and most kinds of spray cans. It also went up to the Earth's atmosphere where it made a huge hole in the ozone layer – the main protection we have from the sun's ultraviolet radiation. Not only that, but a single CFC molecule is around ten thousand times better (or worse, depending on how you look at it) at exacerbating greenhouse effects than a single molecule of carbon dioxide. And CFC molecules generally hang around for more than 100 years. So although CFCs were phased out from commercial use in the 1990s, we'll be suffering the ill effects for generations.

Midgley died in ignorance of all this. In 1940, he contracted polio. Although he was severely disabled, his inventive talent remained with him. One of his last creations was a special harness that took him from his bed to his wheelchair. This was ingenious, but also foolish. In a metaphor for the rest of his career that is near Shakespearean in its poetry, he got caught up in the strings and pulleys of the harness and suffocated.

---

* The fact that these older people were more likely to vote for Trump and Brexit is probably just coincidental.

HENRY FORD

—

Date of birth/death: *30 July 1863 – 7 April 1947*
In a nutshell: *His heart was as black as his cars*
Connected to: *Adolf Hitler*

Who invented the moving assembly line and so enabled mass production and changed the world forever? That's right. It wasn't Henry Ford.

Bicycle manufacturers had been mass-producing their machines on moving lines for decades by the time the first Model T Fords rolled out of the factory. As early as 1881, the Columbia bicycle company was making bikes with interchangeable parts and they started to develop production lines with modern machine tools not long afterwards.* There's even plenty of evidence that Ford, who was a keen

---

* And other kinds of assembly lines had been used for centuries before that. They date at least as far back as Ancient China. Elsewhere, Adam Smith described a mass-produced pin in *The Wealth of Nations*. All kinds of other processes in the Industrial Revolution used more static assembly lines.

cyclist, visited pioneering bicycle plants. He also – cheeringly – knew plenty about the 'disassembly lines' in Chicago's huge abattoirs, where animals were pulled apart in separate stages on conveyor belts. What's more, when Ford factories did make their own assembly lines, it was a collaborative effort rather than the work of Henry Ford alone.*

And yet, somehow, history generally gives Ford himself the credit. It would be wrong to be too cynical. He was a brilliant and creative industrialist who took full advantage of being in the right place at the right time. But it would also be a mistake not to be cynical at all. Especially when it comes to Henry Ford's propaganda.

Ford might have loved riding his bike, but he was never keen to give cyclists any credit for innovation. A good example of his unwillingness to shy away from taking all the credit came in 1927 when he sent out a press release commemorating the 15 millionth Model T to have rolled off the production line and declaring that 'Ford … started the movement for good roads.' This was a lie. The movement to improve the road systems had been a burning issue in both Europe and America for years. And as Ford well knew, the first pressure groups had been started by cycling organisations.

That might seem like a petty point – but it had serious implications. Today the idea that road systems were designed solely for the benefit of motor drivers remains a cultural block when it comes to properly and safely integrating other road users. Meanwhile, Ford's clever promotion of his cars as a lifestyle choice, alongside the fact that he sold 15 million Model T Fords alone, helped ensure that the internal combustion engine has dominated our world for the past century. So if you're worried about our overheating world and if you're breathing

---

* If you believe the memoirs of Charles Sorensen, he and another man called Charlie Lewis provided most of the inventions that made the Ford factories so effective.

poisonous air in a North American or European city (and if you're in a North American or European city, that's almost certainly what you'll be doing), you can direct a good part of your gratitude to Henry Ford.

The motoring pioneer also spread other kinds of poison. In 1918, he bought up a newspaper called *The Dearborn Independent*, which he used to advertise the benefits of his cars – but also to spread repulsive anti-Semitic nonsense. He published article after article referring to shadowy conspiracy theories and blaming every conceivable ill on Jews. He said they were responsible for strikes, for financial scandals, for problems in agriculture, for war – everything. Sample quote: 'If fans wish to know the trouble with American baseball they have it in three words – too much Jew.' The newspaper was distributed at every Ford dealership. If you bought a Model T, chances are that you would find a copy on the seat beside you as you drove out of the dealership. It reached around 700,000 readers. Hitler was one of them. He said that he viewed Ford as his 'inspiration' and kept his picture on his desk.

Ford's charmless editorials were also gathered together in a book wallowing in the title *The International Jew: The World's Foremost Problem*.* At the Nuremberg Trials, Baldur von Schirach, the leader of the Hitler Youth, said: 'I read it and became anti-Semitic. In those days this book made such a deep impression on my friends and myself because we saw in Henry Ford the representative of success.'

So Ford maybe did invent something after all.

---

* Depressingly, the book still appears on anti-Semitic and neo-Nazi websites around the world and has recently been published in Turkey and Egypt.

ADOLF HITLER

Date of birth/death: *20 April 1889 – 30 April 1945*
In a nutshell: *Massive dickhead*
Connected to: *Donald Trump, Steve Bannon, Nigel Farage*

Hitler's final cowardly acts were to order his doctor to test a cyanide capsule on his dog Blondi, to wait for the poor creature to die, to make sure his (secret) wife Eva Braun took a capsule herself, and then to shoot himself in the side of the head. His last ally Benito Mussolini had been shot and strung up by his heels and Hitler was so terrified of meeting a similar fate he ordered his few remaining guards to burn him quickly, before the encircling Russian soldiers could find his corpse.

And when he left the world that he had done so much to harm, he was broken: a drug-addled ruin who heard buzzing in his left ear and had uncontrollable shakes in his left arm. He was defeated: the last few thousand of the old men and boys defending Berlin were soon to surrender. His dreams were rubble and ashes: the Thousand-Year Reich he had promised his people had been crushed.

Above all, he was disgraced, discredited, shamed and abhorred: a byword for murderous insanity, for the slaughter of innocents, for lies and cruelty, for out-of-control rages, for absurd and poisonous anti-Semitism, for hocus-pocus beliefs, for self-delusion and for the gross abuse of power. He was an ogre. A twerp. A perfect perisher. A trumped-up corporal with a daft moustache, a shit haircut and a fetish for uniforms. A joke. A sick and twisted joke. But still a joke.

Except, somehow this villainous failure continues to exert influence today. One of the few books Donald Trump is known to have read is a copy of Hitler's speeches, which he used to keep by his bed. His chief strategist Steve Bannon's Breitbart website has carried articles downplaying the Holocaust by comparing it to Planned Parenthood. Members of the alt-right have been caught on camera shouting 'Hail Trump'. They walk around with Hitler-aping 'fash' clothes and look almost as stupid. And people all over the world continue to use race as a political weapon and push themselves into power.

Hitler's shadow may still loom over us, but it's worth remembering that even if his crimes are too huge and horrible to comprehend, he himself was just a silly little man. A boy who wrote weirdly romantic poems to his mother. A lazy kid, always marked unsatisfactory at school, who became an idle adult. Someone who never did a day's work in his life, who was notorious for spending more time at his holiday home than in Berlin, but who still told his followers: 'I only acknowledge one nobility – that of labour.' Someone who also said, in a rare moment of honesty: 'I have not come into this world to make men better, but to make use of their weaknesses.' But otherwise, someone who lied about his intentions, lied about his actions, lied about their consequences, and lied about his lies about all those things. A man who rambled and ranted and raved from under his crazy hair. Someone who was clearly off his gourd and yet who nobody stopped until it was far too late.

And yes, there is a lesson there that we're failing to heed.

PEPE THE FROG

—

Date of birth: *2005*
In a nutshell: *Fascist frog*
Connected to: *Donald Trump, Adolf Hitler*

It might sound weird to blame the world's ills on a cartoon frog. But then again, if the last few years have shown us anything it's that the world is weird. Catastrophically weird. And Pepe the Frog fits right into that picture.

Pepe began life innocently enough. The artist Matt Furie featured him on the early social network Myspace in 2005 and then in his comic strip Boy's Club. He was just a frog. He sometimes said, 'feels good man' and there was a smug version of him with a supercilious expression that got posted around, and a screaming angry version, and that was really about it. But then, in the unfathomable way of these things, Pepe began to spread further. People began to dress him up. People made Batman Pepe, Borat Pepe, Supermarket Checkout Girl Pepe. Katy Perry tweeted a picture of a crying Pepe when she was suffering from jetlag.

It all seemed innocent. Until late in 2015 when users of politically incorrect message boards on the website 4chan decided to make Pepe their own. They'd show him with swastika eyes. Or next to the numbers 88 (in their world, a symbol for Heil Hitler). And he started popping up on the presidential podium with a red tie around his neck and a crazy yellow bouffant on top of his hair. Because around this time, many of the right-wing and Nazi users of those message boards had also decided to devote themselves to getting Donald Trump elected. They were dedicated internet trolls. Trump meanwhile, with his bizarre tweets, his lies and his ability to get liberals steaming mad, was trolling reality. They called Trump their god-emperor. And they were partly joking. And partly, not so joking.

The 4chan contributors formed a 'Trump army' that used memes to spread its message – and to confuse the hell out of their enemies. They began posting pictures on Twitter of Trump and Pepe together; of Pepe dressed as Trump; and of Pepe next to white nationalist symbols. Presciently, they also spread an image of Hillary Clinton squinting at a computer screen, asking: 'WHO THE HELL IS PEPE?'

By the end of October 2015 Trump himself was retweeting his strange new fans.

And these tweets brought the new, nastier Pepe into the mainstream, along with all the people who were promoting Pepe and all their other variously crazy and persuasive pro-Trump memes.

Political opponents of Trump also began to ask on Twitter about all this business with the green frog. Some warned that he was a white supremacist – and quickly found themselves inundated with Pepe images, many of them sexually explicit and violent. They had broken the first rule of the internet: don't feed the troll. And the trolls grew ever stronger as a result.

Their most glorious moment came on 12 September 2016. A few days earlier, Hillary Clinton had made the fatal mistake of using the term 'deplorables' to describe Donald Trump supporters (which is to say, millions of voters, with millions more friends and family members). Someone at the 4chan meme factory quickly ran up an image based on a poster for the film *The Expendables*. It showed the actors' heads replaced by Donald Trump and his son Donald Trump Jr and also by notorious right-wing trolls like Milo Yiannopolous – and yes, right behind the image of Donald Trump, there was Pepe the Frog.

On 10 September Donald Trump Jr retweeted the image. On 11 September, Hillary Clinton fell over at a memorial event. She was suffering from pneumonia, as it turned out. But Trump's viral army had also been spreading rumours for months that she was too ill to serve as president. So they were already going ballistic about their 'meme-magic' and about everything they posted coming true. And then it happened. Hillary herself fed the troll. On 12 September, a post appeared on her website entitled 'Donald Trump, Pepe the frog, and white supremacists: an explainer'. It had the subheading 'that cartoon frog is more sinister than you might realize'.

There followed a Q&A about Pepe explaining that the frog was a 'symbol associated with white supremacy' and written in faux hipster style:

'Wait. Really? White supremacy?

That's right.

Please explain.

Here's the short version: Pepe is a cartoon frog who began his internet life as an innocent meme enjoyed by teenagers and pop stars alike. But in recent months, Pepe's been almost

entirely co-opted by the white supremacists who call
themselves the 'alt-right.'

Okay, it was damning that Trump and his people should be endorsing such stuff. But the Q&A was not only patronising and ridiculous, it also read exactly like a cranky conspiracy theory. No matter that the Pepe meme really was a bizarre conspiracy and the post was accurate. Clinton had given the trolls everything they wanted. She had served them a slap-up, six-course banquet of absurdity. She had helped their ugly and fascistic fringe movement go mainstream. Pepe started appearing everywhere. Stories about Clinton's illness spread ever wider. All future memes were guaranteed an ever bigger reach. Right-wing radio yukked it up. And people across America saw a presidential candidate walk straight into a trap. They saw that Hillary had taken on a racist cartoon frog – and lost. Suddenly, it didn't seem so strange to think that she might also lose to a reality TV star with crazy hair and extreme ideas about Mexicans …

MARK ZUCKERBERG

—

Date of birth: *14 May 1984*
In a nutshell: *Accidentally anti-social billionaire*
Connected to: *Jeff Bezos, Lynton Crosby, Steve Bannon, Arron Banks*

Mark Zuckerberg might not be a monster. He has pledged to give away a large percentage of his personal fortune. He has spoken up for the rights of threatened minority groups. He has a nice smile and quotes Virgil at meetings. He wears hoodies and looks cuddly.

But Mark Zuckerberg has definitely created a monster. Facebook is destroying our lives.

The social network has grown from a project he launched in his college dorm room in 2004 into one of the biggest and most profitable companies in the world – with all that entails. But this isn't just the usual story of a powerful company controlling huge amounts of information, aggressively avoiding tax, setting up bank accounts in the Cayman Islands, and thus depriving society of the profits it has made from its citizens. The biggest worry about Facebook is the way it can influence everyone and everything. The way it inadvertently channels us into echo chambers of our own social and friendship groups. The way it has allowed some of these groups to post inflammatory and dangerous material. The way it targets still more users to receive still more provocative nonsense.

One of the clearest demonstrations of the problem Facebook poses comes in its moderation policies. The company rarely takes down the pages of fascist groups like the British National Party and the French National Front 'so long as they abide by community rules'. But woe betide anyone who posts a picture of a woman breastfeeding. Racist posts about Muslims can hang around – but nipples disappear within seconds. So long as they belong to fully grown women, anyway. When the BBC investigated secret paedophile groups on Facebook in 2016 they found that the social network was being used to swap suggestive images of children. They reported these and were told that Facebook had thousands of moderators to check such content. The BBC used Facebook's systems to question 100 images. They checked in a year later and found only eighteen had been removed. They approached Facebook about their findings – were asked to forward on the images – and Facebook's legal team reported the BBC to the police. A spokesman explained: 'It's against the law for anyone to distribute images of child exploitation.'

So that's fine.

And one of the many implications of that move is how much it must intimidate anyone else investigating Facebook – especially since the BBC is one of the few mainstream media outlets in the world not reliant on Facebook for advertising revenue. And also apparently one of the few last bastions of non-fake news.

In the final three months of the US election, according to a BuzzFeed survey,* the top twenty false stories from partisan or hoax websites and blogs generated over 8,700,000 likes, shares or comments on Facebook. The top twenty from major mainstream news sites generated 7,367,000 reactions. Maths experts will have realised that that is more than a million fewer.

The top twenty fake stories included the idea that Hillary Clinton sold weapons to ISIS, that tens of thousands of fraudulent Clinton votes had been discovered, that Pope Francis had endorsed Trump for president. You get the idea. They weren't exactly pro-Hillary. And those were just the tip of the iceberg. Facebook's algorithms busily promoted thousands of fake stories on its Trending feature, some of them originating on right-wing sites like Breitbart, some apparently from Russia, some from kids and trolls from as far afield as Macedonia who had realised they could make a quick buck by pumping partisan nonsense into the news ecology.

In December 2016, the anger about the fake news stories that had disfigured the Brexit referendum and then the American presidential election reached such a pitch that Mark Zuckerberg himself put out a public statement. 'Of all the content on Facebook, more than 99 per cent of what people see is authentic,' he said. 'Only a very small amount is fake news and hoaxes. The hoaxes that do exist are not limited to one partisan view, or even to politics. Overall, this makes it extremely unlikely hoaxes changed the outcome of this election in one direction or the other.'

---

* In case you were wondering – and why wouldn't you? – this survey is credible, well sourced and checkable. You can find it here: https://www.buzzfeed.com/craigsilverman/viral-fake-election-news-outperformed-real-news-on-facebook?utm_term=.rxq32odo4#.aralygegb

But people on the Trump team were suggesting otherwise. Trump campaign digital director Brad Parscale told BuzzFeed News: 'Facebook was the single most important platform to help grow our fundraising base.' Other campaign staffers also tweeted about how crucial Facebook was to the Trump campaign.

Across the Atlantic, UK campaigners were similarly buoyant about their ability to use Facebook for political ends. In the 2015 election, the Conservative Party spent in excess of £100,000 per month on Facebook advertising alone, with Lynton Crosby's team constantly tracking responses, dropping ads that didn't work, pushing those that did ever harder into the communities that responded to them.

But it was the Leave campaign in the 2016 referendum who did the most to lift the lid on Facebook's frightening potential. Andy Wigmore (the Brexit campaigner who took the infamous photo of Nigel Farage and Donald Trump grinning in a golden elevator) said that a Facebook 'like' was Leave.EU's most 'potent weapon'.

Wigmore said there was more to it than just fake news. 'It's creepy! It's really creepy! It's why I'm not on Facebook,' he told the *Observer*. He explained his campaign had artificial-intelligence systems that would tell them what sort of advert to use with different individuals – and then find the other people in those individuals' networks and follow them and target them – and so on.

Companies like a UK-based organisation called Cambridge Analytica gathered information on both sides of the Atlantic that enabled campaign teams to hit people with tailored adverts designed to change voter behaviour. The theory was that they could gauge people's emotional personality type and interests based on the things they had 'liked' on Facebook, alongside data they gleaned from the website about their age and family and place of residence, and target them accordingly. Election campaigns even sent 'dark posts' persuading people not to vote. Inhabitants of the Miami District of Little Haiti, who might have voted for Clinton, were sent adverts about her foundation's supposed failures to help with an earthquake. Both pro-Brexit and Trump campaigners were also given an app called Groundgame that provided them with data about which doors to knock on, according to how receptive the people inside were likely to be to their message.

Facebook, in short, was enabling political campaigns to carry out bio-psycho profiling – or 'cognitive warfare', as it's since become known. And it all sounds almost too strange to believe. Not least because so far, most of the evidence about Facebook's ability to swing elections comes from people claiming to have used dodgy adverts and fake news stories to their advantage. People who are thereby simultaneously confessing themselves to be bullshit merchants.

There is, however, a reliable source about Facebook's ability to change election outcomes. And yes, that source is a well-known social media platform called Facebook. Not long after the 2016 election, Facebook posted a story on their business pages boasting about using 'an audience specific content strategy' to help the Republican Senator Pat Toomey get over the line and win his seat. They quoted a digital agency worker called Amanda Bloom explaining that: 'With Facebook's variety of targeting capabilities, we were able to reach more than 1.2 million people with content that was customized to the audience as well as Facebook's platform.' They posted information about how Toomey's marketing team were able to reach voters 'most likely to re-elect' Senator Toomey and said that the campaign achieved double-digit 'uplifts' in voter intent.

Pretty impressive figures! Facebook must be really good at this stuff. Small wonder that in his personal statement Mark Zuckerberg also said: 'Overall, I am proud of our role giving people a voice in this election.'

According to a 2009 survey in the UK, roughly 20 per cent of divorce
petitions contained a reference to Facebook.

ARRON BANKS

—

Date of birth: *22 March 1966*
In a nutshell: *Claims not to work for Putin. Not everyone believes him.*
Connected to: *Mark Zuckerberg, Steve Bannon, Nigel Farage, Donald Trump,*
Vladimir Putin

Pretty much the first time Arron Banks appeared in the national press in the UK was as a footnote to someone else's story.

This was a mucky and murky scandal uncovered in 2010 about a Liberal Democrat MP called Mike Hancock. Hancock was facing questions because MI5 had arrested his mistress and parliamentary aide Katia Zatuliveter as an espionage agent. It turned out that while Hancock had been taking a determinedly pro-Putin line as chair of the All-Party Parliamentary Russia Group, he had also been entertaining a string of Russian and Ukrainian women. He had also helped a young lady from Russia called Ekaterina Paderina to stay in the UK after she ran into visa problems in the late 1990s. She appeared in the *Daily Telegraph* in an article about the later 'Russian "spy" case'. That *Telegraph* story also contained a sentence that would take on new resonance following FBI director James Comey's suggestion that Putin supported Brexit. It said simply that in November 2001, Ekaterina married 'millionaire insurance company director Arron Banks'.*

The Conservative MP William Hague unfortunately missed this reference. So when Arron Banks announced he was leaving the Tory party and was giving £100,000 to Nigel Farage's UKIP in 2014, Hague went on the radio to describe Banks as 'somebody we haven't heard of'. Banks decided to give UKIP £1 million instead. 'Now he knows who I am,' he told journalists.

Since then, Banks has made sure no one else can forget about him either. He is, as the papers call him, 'the man who bought Brexit'. That £1 million gift to UKIP turned out to be only the beginning. Banks – a man who had started out selling vacuum cleaners door-to-door ('I was quite good at persuading people to buy things they didn't want to buy'), and went on to make a fortune running and selling insurance companies – was soon pumping millions of pounds into a group called Leave.EU, and masterminding some of the most successful elements of the Brexit campaign.

He was also soon enjoying a long boozy lunch with the Russian ambassador,† and went on the record to talk about his admiration for Vladimir Putin and his 'strength as a politician'. But that was probably just coincidence. What we have on the record is the fact that Banks engaged the Washington campaign strategy firm Goddard Gunster, who told him that the major issue in the EU referendum was

---

* Ekatarina was never formally accused of being a spy. But one of Banks' Range Rovers once had the number plate X MI5 SPY.

† In his book *The Bad Boys of Brexit*, Banks explained that the ambassador produced a 'special surprise': a bottle of vodka the ambassador claimed was one of only three from a batch made personally for Joseph Stalin.

immigration – and that he should exploit it. The week after the UK voted to leave the EU, Banks triumphantly explained: 'What they said early on was, "Facts don't work," and that's it. The Remain campaign featured fact, fact, fact, fact, fact. It just doesn't work. You have got to connect with people emotionally. It's the Trump success.'

Leave.EU had made this connection by pumping out post-fact videos, text messages, cartoons, tweets and Facebook posts.* 'Are you worried about the overcrowding of the UK and the burden on the NHS?' asked one video. 'Are you concerned about the amount of crime being committed in the UK by foreign criminals? Isn't it time to take back control?' Other tweets and 'news' stories referenced David Cameron's (non-existent) plans to give '75 million Turks access' to the NHS. Or urged readers to 'act' before 'Islamic extremism' brought about another 'atrocity' like the one that had recently been seen in a nightclub in Orlando. Notoriously, the campaign also quoted a British general's doubts about the EU – while neglecting to mention that the quotes were taken from an article in which he had said he supported the Remain side.

'We used their own words but picked the bits we wanted,' Banks told the *New Statesman*. He spent a lot of time after the campaign speaking to journalists about his similarly clever ways of winning votes. At last, his name was well known. Pro-Remain MP William Hague probably cursed him nightly. And Banks kept his profile up in other ways. He described UKIP as an organisation run by 'circus clowns'. He tweeted that he was 'sick to death' of hearing about the Hillsborough football tragedy. He was also one of the first people to go and meet Donald Trump following his own electoral success, enjoying Trump's golden hospitality even before Nigel Farage.

---

* Banks was instrumental in employing the services of Cambridge Analytica, the organisation also used by the Trump campaign to help them send targeted messages to Facebook users.

Banks again hit the headlines when he was accused of being one of the 'Kremlin's Trojan horses' in a report by the Atlantic Council released in November 2016. Banks described that as 'a sad little conspiracy which would be completely laughable if it wasn't such an insult to the millions of ordinary people who are responsible for this modern revolution'. And with his record for trustworthiness, who could doubt him?

NIGEL FARAGE

—

Date of birth: *3 April 1964*
In a nutshell: *Stilton-brained man-sized bollock*
Connected to: *Vladimir Putin, Donald Trump, Steve Bannon*

Aside from being the kind of yellow-trousered eggburp who calls barmen 'squire', our pound shop mini-Hitler has worked tirelessly to coarsen UK political life and stir up racial hatred. 'We are changing the national debate in this country,' Nigel Farage told the BBC in 2013, 'and that for me makes it worthwhile getting up in the morning.'

And it's thanks to Farage's unfortunate habit of waking up every day that the UK has become a country where Muslims are attacked and insulted on public transport. Where our European friends and co-workers feel afraid for their future and residency status – and also, often have to endure attacks and insults just for talking their own language. Where MPs who promote tolerance are shot and stabbed in the street by right-wing freaks shouting 'Britain first!'

Farage has helped us make this shift to intolerance with a smile on his face, red wine in his belly and, as he describes it, 'exuberance'. But he's still done it. Mainly by stealth, repeatedly exaggerating the threats and costs of immigration, and making subtle appeals to Little English nationalism. Sometimes more directly. Every so often, he reveals a chink in his ... Actually, let's not use the word 'chink'. He has made it rancid. 'If you and your mates were going out for a Chinese, what do you say you're going for?' asked Farage in an infamous interview. When the presenter told him he wouldn't ever use the slur 'chink', Farage said: 'A lot would.'

Such appeals to the many, to the malevolent and insular volk are Farage's stock in trade, along with vague hints about things 'you' know to be true. 'I was asked, if a group of Romanian men moved in next to you, would you be concerned? And if you lived in London, I think you would be,' he once told LBC radio listeners. Asked if he would have similar objections to German children he said: 'You know the difference.'

It doesn't really matter if we 'know the difference' or not. What we do know is what Farage is implying. He doesn't have to spell it out. Just hint broadly enough. Like the time he blamed the fact that he was late for a meeting in Port Talbot on immigrants, saying 'the M4 is not as navigable as it used to be' because the country is too full. Or like the time he said that it would be a 'good start' if HIV sufferers were not allowed to come to the UK. Or the time he said he felt 'uncomfortable' when people spoke other languages on the train. And the time when he said: 'Our real friends in the world speak English, have common law, and stand by us in times of crisis.'

Poor 'the national debate'. It's also had to suffer such indignities as a wakeful Farage saying that women shouldn't be 'openly ostentatious' about breastfeeding their children and should perhaps 'sit in a corner'. Also, his suggestion that it's okay that women are paid less because they are 'worth far less' than their male counterparts: 'A woman who has a client base, has a child and takes two or three years off – she is worth far less to her employer when she comes back than when she went away because that client base won't be stuck as rigidly to her portfolio.'

Farage managed to go even lower during the European Referendum campaign when he presented a poster of a snaking queue of Middle Eastern men on which were written the words: 'Breaking Point', and 'We must break free of the EU and take back control of our borders.'

The poster was eerily reminiscent of a visual the Nazis used of Jewish refugees in the 1930s.

Farage said: 'This is a photograph – an accurate, undoctored photograph – taken on 15 October last year … frankly, as you can see from this picture, most of the people coming are young males and, yes, they may be coming from countries that are not in a very happy state, they may be coming from places that are poorer than us, but the EU has made a fundamental error that risks the security of everybody.'

What he didn't say is that the photograph was actually taken in Slovenia and none of the young men – who were fleeing a war zone – were queuing to get into Britain.

This poster was unveiled on the morning the MP Jo Cox was shot and stabbed. A few days later, after Britain voted to leave Europe, Farage said that it was done 'without a bullet being fired'. He said that even before Jo Cox was buried.

Farage has continued this charm assault post-Brexit. He's threatened that there will be riots if the referendum result is not enforced. He's praised Donald Trump for 'dominating' Hillary Clinton like a 'silverback gorilla'. He's defended Trump's assertion that you should 'grab' women by the 'pussy' as 'alpha-male boasting'. Unsurprisingly, given his long-standing links with Trump's chief strategist Steve Bannon (not to mention his many appearances on the Kremlin's Russia Today TV channel), Farage also quickly declared that he 'couldn't be happier' that Trump won the 2016 election. He did still manage to shock the world, however, when he called outgoing President Barack Obama a 'loathsome individual' and referred to 'that Obama creature'.

A couple of months later, Farage became embroiled in a row about a knighthood. Farage has always liked to claim that he is an anti-establishment figure, on the side of the people, and not a career politician like all the rest. Which is a rather counter-intuitive stance for the wealthy son of a stockbroker, who went to Dulwich College, an expensive public school, before becoming a stockbroker himself and then spending over twenty years in frontline politics. It's also a strange thing to claim for someone so cringingly keen on bagging himself a 'K'. Emails leaked to the *Daily Telegraph* showed discussions among UKIP members about lobbying for either a peerage or knighthood for Farage and asking UKIP's one MP, Douglas Carswell, to approach the government chief whip to appeal when the bid was turned down. Carswell's reply was leaked too: 'As promised, I did speak to the government chief whip. Perhaps we might try angling to get Nigel an OBE next time round? For services to headline writers? An MBE, maybe? Let's discuss.'

The hilarity didn't end there. Farage also appeared again on Russia Today, where a small girl was wheeled on screen to enact a symbolic knighthood for the great man. After she had dubbed his shoulders with a plastic sword the girl declared: 'My mummy says you hate foreigners.'

Alas, poor Farage. Even little girls pick on him. Carswell does too. Farage said of the knighthood exchanges that they showed Carswell was 'consumed with jealousy and a desire to hurt me'. It's hard to be Nigel. He once explained on Irish radio: 'If you challenge consensus, whether it's in science, politics or business, all through the ages of man the first technique is to try and laugh you off for being a bunch of nutcases. They did it to Galileo, they did it to Darwin, they did it to O'Leary from Ryanair. This is how it works. So to be mocked and derided is not unusual.'

O'Leary is the man who helped bring low-cost airlines to the world. Darwin, among other things, came up with the theory of evolution. Galileo confirmed the transits of Venus and insisted the world was round. And Nigel Farage picked on minority groups, was rude to our friends in Europe and said appalling things about women. But, he insists, he is the one who is hard done by. 'I've had twenty years of abuse,' he complained to the Conservative Political Action Conference in the USA in February 2017. He was speaking not long after Donald Trump and just one night before he was also photographed having dinner with the billionaire president. But still. Poor Nigel. Perpetually the victim. If only he'd stayed in bed.

In 1981, a teacher at Dulwich College sent a letter to the headmaster about plans to make Farage a prefect. She included a note from one master who said that Farage was 'a fascist, but that was no reason why he would not make a good prefect'. (No one said Dulwich wasn't weird.) She also wrote: 'Another colleague, who teaches the boy, described his publicly professed racist and neo-fascist views; and he cited a particular incident in which Farage was so offensive to a boy in his set, that he had to be removed from the lesson.' She warned too that another teacher had seen Farage marching through a Sussex village 'shouting Hitler Youth songs'. When the letter was printed in the *Independent* newspaper Farage admitted only to being annoying at school and said he knew no Hitler Youth songs 'in English or German'. But another pupil later wrote in anonymously to the paper to say that he too remembered Farage singing such material. One song started: 'Gas them all, gas 'em all, gas them all'.

JAMES GOLDSMITH

Date of birth/death: *26 February 1933 – 18 July 1997*
In a nutshell: *Corrupt businessman and conspiracy theorist. Weird in the 1990s*
– but normal for now.
Connected to: *Nigel Farage, Margaret Thatcher, Ronald Reagan*

James Goldsmith was a populist campaigner who headed a campaign to leave the European Union early in the 1990s. He was also a sickeningly rich and well-connected conman. It may or may not surprise you to learn that the UK press has labelled him 'the man who was Farage before there was Nigel Farage'.

Goldsmith first became notorious during the 1980s when he used his considerable wealth to pioneer a business technique known as 'greenmail'. This shady practice was handily defined by Goldsmith himself in one of his many court appearances: 'If,' he said, 'a company or an individual buys shares of a company with the specific purpose of frightening management so as to put management into using corporate funds to protect their position by buying back that block at unusually favourable terms, then I would call that person a greenmailer.'

This description could easily apply to Goldsmith's own actions in 1983 when he and a partnership bought £3 million worth of shares in the St Regis Corporation and then offered to buy out the rest of the company at $52 a share. The chairman of St Regis, who wanted to keep control of the company himself, decided he had to buy Goldsmith's stake in the company back from him at the same price. Goldsmith and his backers made $51 million. Not bad for a month's work.

Okay, it probably wasn't 'good' work either, but for a while, it seemed win–win for Goldsmith. He would either end up buying a company he fancied asset-stripping, or make a fat profit out of thin air. So he kept at it. Most famously, in 1986 he went for the Goodyear Tire and Rubber Company, buying 1.7 million shares at $33 each. When he was revealed as the buyer, the share price immediately rose to $48. Goldsmith continued to accumulate shares. When he had more than 10 per cent of the company, he offered to buy the rest for $49 a share. Goodyear resisted – and the deal became the subject of huge controversy. So much so that the US government got involved. Goldsmith was made to explain himself at a hearing at the House of Representatives in Washington. He was jeered at and heckled by crowds outside. When he was inside, things didn't go much better. A Congressman asked Goldsmith 'Who the hell are you?' and applause broke out. Goldsmith gurned and frowned and ranted during his defence. When he watched the tapes back, even he was surprised at how nasty he seemed. 'I look like a monster, it's incredible,' he said. (At least he got the first bit right.)

But even after this brief moment of self-awareness, Goldsmith was unbowed. He took a quick break to host a dinner given in honour of US President Ronald Reagan, and then sold his shares for $620 million – thus netting himself a cool $93 million. After this scandal, moves were made to tighten regulations. Former business associates and fellow corporate raiders of Goldsmith's like Ivan Boesky were also starting to get arrested – and spill the beans on their more questionable techniques. Goldsmith decided to retreat, not least because he also didn't like the look of the markets. He liquidated all his holdings just days before Black Monday on 19 October 1987. *Time* magazine even put him on the cover, describing him as the 'Lucky Gambler'. With characteristic charisma, Goldsmith told them that he wouldn't go back to the markets unless in a very special situation: 'Like the scorpion in La Fontaine's fable, I may be tempted to sting ... just because I like to sting.'

By the 1990s Goldsmith had also found somewhere else to direct his poison. During that disastrous hearing in the House of Representatives, he had started accusing his American listeners of having 'the European disease'. Cheerfully misquoting Milton Friedman, he railed against big business, big unions and big governments, suggesting that the safe and egalitarian societies in Europe were uniquely dangerous.

He had long harboured a dislike of Europe and this became his dominant theme. In 1994 he turned up on the David Frost TV programme, and offered £20 million to any party that would stand candidates asking for a referendum. He then went even further and set up his own party, the Referendum Party. The party held its first (and last) conference in 1996. Speakers made speeches about resisting 'conquest' and the 'five great tribes' in England – 'the Angles, the Jutes, the Normans, the Saxons and the Danes'. (That's right, there wasn't even room for the Celts.) Goldsmith started getting increasingly excited. He next pumped his ill-gotten gains into campaigning at the 1997 General Election campaign. Among other costly propaganda operations, he sent a VHS tape to five million homes. It promised to tell the 'truth' about Europe, and naturally, it was jammed with all the conspiracies about a super-state and 'career politicians' that would become so familiar over the next twenty years. During a maniacally staring piece to camera, Goldsmith promised, 'a referendum will heal the deep divisions that run right through the nation'. Oh well.

Goldsmith himself stood at the 1997 election – and lost his deposit. As the results were announced he started screaming at the outgoing Conservative MP David Mellor. As Mellor conceded defeat to the winning Labour candidate, he also observed that Goldsmith's Referendum party was 'dead in the water'. He was right. They never fought another election. They were a laughing stock. But many of the newly radicalised members went on to join another new organisation, the UK Independence Party. And no one's laughing any more.

Margaret Thatcher was one of Goldsmith's close friends. Of course she was. 'Jimmy Goldsmith was one of the most powerful and dynamic personalities that this generation has seen,' she said after his death. 'He was enormously generous.'

RAY KROC

———

Date of birth/death: *5 October 1902 – 14 January 1984*
In a nutshell: *Cows feared him, tycoons wanted to be him*
Connected to: *Jeff Bezos*

The McDonald's chain was first established by two brothers called Richard and Maurice McDonald. They had a few busy restaurants in the San Bernardino area of California – and they pioneered the Speedee Service System that allowed them to chuck out burger meals quickly and with impressive uniformity. And if that had been the end of the story, their good name would probably have endured for a few years after their prosperous and calorie-rich deaths and then faded into history.

It took Ray Kroc to make them notorious.

Kroc was a fifty-two-year-old almost down-and-out when he first encountered the McDonald brothers in 1955. He was a travelling salesman hawking a failing product: an overpriced milkshake mixer. His stroke of good fortune came because the brothers had bought an unusually large number of Kroc's mixers for their restaurants and he went to visit them to find out why. He saw their speedy delivery service and tasted their burgers and realised that they had invented a formula for global domination.

Global domination for Ray Kroc, anyway. The brothers weren't particularly interested in rapid expansion, even after Kroc persuaded them to let him become their franchising agent and raked in huge profits to prove how well their system worked. But Kroc eventually persuaded the brothers to allow him to buy up the chain lock, stock and barrel. He gave them $2.7 million dollars – enough for $1 million each after tax. He also promised them an annual royalty of 1.9 per cent (because the brothers thought 2 per cent sounded too greedy).

You might be thinking that almost 2 per cent of McDonald's annual profits might amount to a pretty generous sum – but if you are, you haven't reckoned on Ray Kroc. The deal was worked out on a spit and a handshake – and not on paper. So Kroc never paid Richard and Maurice their royalties. To further prove his good nature, he also opened a McDonald's near the brothers' original – then forced them to change the name of their restaurant to the 'Big M' because he'd also got himself full rights to their name.

Yes, the Big M went out of business. And after that Kroc really let rip on his evil McVillain persona. He began to advertise heavily to children using the sinister clown Ronald McDonald, reasoning that kids would always bring their parents into restaurants with them – and that the young innocents would become lifelong dependents. He also began to insist on pesticide-heavy farming methods and aggressive expansion, while – like so many capitalist-ultras before and since – loudly moaning about government and union interference.

Kroc's drive and ruthless ambition was typified by the aggressive, anti-educational inspirational quote from Calvin Coolidge* that he hung in every restaurant kitchen:

> *Nothing in the world can take the place of persistence. Talent will not; nothing is more common than unsuccessful men with talent. Genius will not; unrewarded genius is almost a proverb. Education will not; the world is full of educated derelicts. Persistence and determination alone are omnipotent.*

Thanks to this relentless persistence, McDonald's is one of the world's most recognisable names. But it is also one of the most maligned. The restaurants under the golden arches of that famous 'M' have provided affordability and familiarity to millions around the world. But for many, McDonald's has become a symbol of the greed and corruption of the capitalist system. Over the years the food chain has been associated with the destruction of rainforests, factory farming, cruelty to animals, the overuse of pesticides and shrinking biodiversity. The brand has also been accused of contributing to the global obesity epidemic. And it has come to symbolise wage stagnation and the exploitation of workers. 'McJob' has become a derogatory term, as has Mc-just-about-everything-else. There may be some justice in many of these accusations, but the McDonald's name itself has been unfairly maligned. Kroc is the real crook.

---

* The 30th US president and the man who helped foster the conditions necessary for the 1929 stock market crash.

JEFF BEZOS

—

Date of birth: 12 January 1964
In a nutshell: One click and you're done for
Connected to: Ray Kroc, Mark Zuckerberg, Hal 9000

One of the early names Jeff Bezos thought of using for Amazon was Relentless.com. It was a name that embodied his personality and philosophy – a tireless, persistent urge to build bigger, better and faster. To laser-focus on customer satisfaction. To work harder and longer than almost anyone else on the planet.

Relentless instead became the brand name for a drink containing scary amounts of caffeine. Bezos himself just became more and more scary. The fact that he is now one of the world's richest billionaires with his own space programme* – is a measure of his success. Of how much we should fear him. And of how close he is to becoming a real-life James Bond villain.

---

* He is funding a system of travel outside Earth's orbit and fully intends to use it. He's sending himself to space. He's that ambitious.

Like many of Bond's best opponents, Bezos is supremely intelligent, not to mention a superb businessman. He's changed the way the world shops, consumes media and even the way it thinks. That we now expect instant access to any product we want is largely thanks to Jeff Bezos and his everything store.

But Amazon's success has come at a price – for everyone else. Amazon has always argued that it's in the nature of technology to disrupt traditional industries – and that those who are against them are against the future. But the problem doesn't arise from their technological innovations, so much as the way they are used. Luddites have always been misrepresented. Even in the good old machine-breaking days, King Ludd and his followers weren't objecting to the new equipment in the mills they worked in, so much as the way their bosses were using them to lower wages and ruin their lives. Likewise, the trouble with Amazon isn't that they make interesting gadgets. It's the way that they use them.

Back in the days when it was mainly a bookstore, Amazon had a programme called the Gazelle Project. So-called because, as Bezos had said in a meeting, the aim was to pursue small publishers like a cheetah would a sickly gazelle. Amazon started to use the fact that they had a near monopoly on backlist sales to leverage ever deeper discounts from their helpless prey. They then graduated to treating bigger companies with similar ruthlessness. Amazon has used bookselling as a Trojan horse to gather up user metadata, build up users and bust into hundreds of other sectors, building up a huge customer database and ever more capital to give it tremendous market power. Several times in the past Amazon has taken huge losses to undercut its competitors on price and force them into selling up. To Amazon.

There are other prices associated with Amazon's cost-cutting. In 2014 the International Trade Union Conference gave Bezos the not-at-all-coveted World's Worst Boss Award in recognition of his 'inhumanity'.

It isn't just that Amazon has prevented its staff from unionising, with its associated benefits. Even executives have been reported to have left the company suffering from post-traumatic stress disorder thanks to gruelling workloads and the moral challenges associated with working for the company. And towards the bottom of the supply chain, in the vast order-fulfilment warehouses, have come the horror stories. There have been reports about Amazon hiring private ambulances to wait outside while workers toiled away during heatwaves,* and others about low-paid workers sleeping outside warehouses in tents during December in Scotland in 2016. This latter because they wanted to save travel costs and were so fearful of missing shifts. Inside that warehouse, meanwhile, working conditions were said to be 'intolerable', with huge pressure to meet targets, penalties for taking sick days and water fountains running empty, even though workers had to walk up to ten miles a day.

Meanwhile, the multi-billion-pound company has become notorious for avoiding taxes. In 2015 Amazon registered £6.3 billion in sales and paid just £9.8 million in tax in the UK. Over the years it has been similarly successful at minimising its bills around the world. And so it is that Amazon has also helped unpick the fabric of our society. It isn't just that it has put so many thousands of independent retailers out of business, eaten into the profits of several major industries and built itself dangerous monopolistic powers. It's that it has deprived us all of money we could be using on essential services. It has undermined the strength of our democracies. It has added to the feeling that we are cut off and detached from the centres of power. To the feeling that while we're left scrabbling around on the increasingly hard and dirty ground our hard-earned money is being used to blast billionaire playboys into orbit. But hey! At least you don't have to leave the

---

* This happened in 2011 in Lehigh Valley. Eventually an emergency room doctor called in federal regulators.

house to buy Ayn Rand books, butt plugs or Nicolas Cage pillowcases.

Brad Stone's book *The Everything Store* gave the world a formidable list of Jeff Bezos' best insults. Questions he's asked his employees include:

- Are you lazy or just incompetent?
- Why are you ruining my life?
- Do we have the right people working on this? (Said to the people who had just handed him a proposal.)
- Do I need to go down and get the certificate that says I'm the CEO of the company to stop you challenging me on this?
- This document was clearly written by the B team. Can someone get me the A team document? I don't want to waste my time with the B team document.

HAL 9000

—

Date of birth: *2001*
In a nutshell: *Robots and algorithms are going to own us all*
Connected to: *Mark Zuckerberg, Jeff Bezos*

We all know that robots are going to destroy us. We're all too aware that our metal-hearted overlords are about to inflict annihilation. We've seen *Terminator 2*.

We also know that there's already a machine that can beat chess grandmasters. That computers are so complex that no one human can understand how each part works. That they can only be built with the help of other computers. Worse than that, that there are now advanced artificial intelligence systems that are being used to develop yet more advanced artificial intelligence systems, because our own paltry intelligence just isn't up to the job.

We know, in short, that we've made machines that can learn and then make better versions of themselves. But we don't know why we did it. What possessed us to make these robots? Why fill the world with machines that can shoot all kinds of explosives at us? That can set off nuclear bombs? And doesn't it worry us that there still isn't one that can make a decent omelette? And that we don't know how to pull out the plug?

And the worst thing is that by now we've had proof that no Arnold Schwarzenegger will come back from the future to stop all this madness. Because if that were going to happen, someone would surely also have come back to get rid of Donald Trump …

Anyway, the thing I'm trying to say is: we're screwed. And not only in the sci-fi robot future. We're in trouble now and we can direct a big part of the blame at our robot friends. More specifically, we can blame the algorithms behind many of their functions.

Briefly, an algorithm is a set of rules that robots or computers follow in calculations and other problem-solving operations. The thinking robot in *2001: A Space Odyssey* gets its name HAL 9000, for instance, because it is a **H**euristically* programmed **AL**gorithmic computer. To put it in more practical terms, it's algorithms that help Google find search results, that enable online stores to recommend you items based on your previous shopping, that start feeding you adverts for meeting up with 'mature women' as soon as you reach your 40th birthday.

It was also algorithms that helped spread all that fake news into the news streams of people around the world during the nightmarish US election of 2016. It's algorithms that direct us to articles we didn't know we wanted to read, but which we inevitably discover feed right into our prejudices …

---

* Heuristic is a method of quick problem-solving in computer science. It refers to a method of problem-solving based on ranking alternative choices in the data algorithms provide. (Roughly!)

And if that isn't frightening enough, algorithms are even getting alarmingly good at writing these articles for themselves. There are programs out there that use a three-part formula based on potential ad results, search terms and other media activity to feed into an algorithm that – with minimal human assistance – chucks out headlines and copy written in suitable language to encourage clicks. There are even programs that can take the various statistics generated in baseball matches and then churn out passable match reports. There are programs that can turn press releases into stories. And gossip.

That's right! They're coming for the writers! These monstrous things have the potential to put people like me out of a job.

Algorithms also have the potential to take out most of the other achingly middle-class professions in the modern world. You'd think, for instance, that wine-tasters might be safe from our robot-overlords. But this is not so. Because algorithmic formulae can predict wine quality. In the 1980s, a Princeton University economist called Orley Ashenfelter started claiming that: wine quality = $12.145 + 0.00117$ winter rainfall $+ 0.0614$ average growing season temperature $- 0.00386$ harvest rainfall. He'd plug in weather statistics, set the algorithms running and then publish his results in a newsletter called Liquid Assets. *Wine* magazine said that he was 'self-evidently silly'. Respected wine buffs mocked him, suggesting he was like a critic who didn't go and see a film but judged it on the basis of actor and director. He was openly derided when he said the 1989 Bordeaux vintage would be the best on record. And then when he claimed the 1990 would be even better, many wine magazines stopped carrying his adverts. It was only ten years later that everyone realised he had been right.

There are also parametrically controlled* designs in architecture. More and more accountancy functions can be performed by algorithms. Solicitors. Bookmakers. The robots are getting an ever-greater grip on the world of work from top to bottom. Walmart have come up with a system of hiring people based on personality types checked by algorithms rather than through interviews. Meanwhile, millions – billions – of stock market trades are carried out by algorithms.†

So be scared. Go on. Even if you're thinking that there's plenty that you can do that robotic number-crunchers won't be able to do. Just as office clerks were replaced by calculators and spreadsheets, so the chances are your job isn't as secure as you might think either. Worse still, that's not really the point. The point isn't that algorithms can do your job better. The point is that they can find a way to make money where you can't. They can find targets that you will never be able to find and they can hit them. Few people are likely to enjoy an article written by a robot better than a piece by Charles Dickens. But they are far more likely to click on one. So too is your racist Facebook acquaintance … As we've all learned to our cost.

_____

* The basic idea is that you can codify all the design constraints and considerations into mathematical parameters so that you can then theoretically throw a blob of architecture stuff into the algorithmic mesh, adjust a few knobs and watch it expand, curl, shrink and overhang to create a form in harmony with its constraints. But thinking about it too much makes my brain ache.

† And they frequently mess up. In late 2016, for instance, when sterling was already taking a pummelling because of Brexit, they caused a flash crash that knocked 8 per cent off its value – before jolting it back to previous levels 30 minutes later.

JULIAN ASSANGE

—

Date of birth: *3 July 1971*
In a nutshell: *Creepy web crawler*
Connected to: *Vladimir Putin, Nigel Farage, Donald Trump*

One of the many worries of our age is that we are merely living through a preposterous film script. The connections between Brexit and Trump, Trump and Putin, Putin and Brexit seem too absurd to believe. As do the villains. Who in their right mind would have dreamed up Donald Trump, with his dog-bum mouth ranting away beneath all that crazy hair? Who would have set Steve Bannon brooding behind him, like a giant and angry piece of pork scratching? Who would have bothered to have Nigel Farage toadying his way into their parties, gurning in a golden lift? And how to explain Michael Gove?

But it's when Julian Assange slithers onto the scene that things get most ludicrous. That this pallid, predatory, smoothly spoken fugitive from justice should somehow join all the dots. That he should do so using computers inside the Ecuadorian Embassy, where he's been hiding for half a decade after fleeing charges for sex crimes … It's too much. And yet. Here we are.

Few would have predicted back in 2006 that Assange would be widely believed to be acting for the secretive authoritarian Russian government in order to help bring Donald Trump into power. When he helped set up WikiLeaks in 2006, ostensibly to allow whistle-blowers to release official documents, he was generally popular among liberals. Never more so than following the 2010 release of information provided by an American army intelligence analyst called Chelsea Manning. The footage of unarmed Iraqis being gunned down by US helicopters shocked the world. WikiLeaks also released fascinating material about the war in Afghanistan, revealing documents from the Church of Scientology and much more that seemed important. Assange was often hailed as a hero. He was supported by the usual suspects on the left like Jeremy Corbyn, Oliver Stone and Michael Moore. And if he was also praised by Russian President Dmitry Medvedev, well, why not? Assange was breaking new ground.

There were clear ethical questions about what Assange was doing. He was testing the boundaries of state secrecy. There were potential risks to people named in the materials he released, not to mention the danger that intelligence operatives might have their cover blown. But those dismissing Assange as a foreign agent and a terrorist were generally seen as hysterics.

In his pomp, in 2010, he said in an interview with Ted Media: 'It's a worry, isn't it, that the rest of the world's media is doing such a bad job that a little group of activists is able to release more of that type of information than the rest of the world press combined.'

No one asked just how worrying it was … And perhaps if we had we wouldn't be where we are now.

One of the early big hints that things were starting to get strange came in August 2010 after Assange went home with two women after a party in Sweden. One of the women said she had been raped, and the other that she had been molested and coerced. Assange was allowed to leave the country, but soon Sweden's special prosecutor wanted to talk to him.

He didn't want to talk to her. There began a long game of cat and mouse, with Assange claiming that the Swedish authorities really just wanted to catch him so they could send him to the USA so he could face spying charges. Eventually, he sought asylum in the Ecuadorian embassy in 2012. He knew the Ecuadorian President Rafael Correa was a fan of WikiLeaks because he'd repeatedly praised the organisation during an interview on Assange's TV show on Russia Today.

We need to pause here. In 2012, Assange had also started running a TV show on Vladimir Putin's propaganda outlet Russia Today, a channel dedicated to singing the praises of the Russian regime and undermining everyone else. It didn't look good back then. In retrospect, it looks positively alarming.

By this time too, Nigel Farage's UKIP party had started to court Assange. Subsequently, leaked emails have shown that UKIP repeatedly reached out to Assange with offers of help to fight the European arrest warrant that had been taken out against him. The MEP Gerard Batten even called for the European Parliament to debate his arrest. Batten then appeared on – yes – Russia Today and branded attempts to extradite Assange 'legalised kidnap'.

Murky as all that might have been, it was only really in 2016 that the extent of Assange's links with Putin became a burning hot issue. Assange set about apparently doing everything he could to undermine Hillary Clinton. WikiLeaks began to release more and more emails hacked from the Democratic National Committee and senior officials in her campaign, generally timed to cause maximum embarrassment whenever she was ahead in the polls. The leaks were soon linked to the Russian state by the US intelligence community – but it didn't take espionage geniuses to work out what had happened. Donald Trump himself had publicly called on Russia to launch espionage operations against Hillary. Many of the documents WikiLeaks released even had giveaway Russian codes on them – and, hilariously, handwriting in Russian script.

Meanwhile, it was also becoming increasingly obvious that WikiLeaks had nothing to say about Trump, and had been weirdly silent about Putin for years and years. Eventually even the Ecuadorians became too embarrassed and cut off Assange's internet connection.

Assange himself continued to deny he had any links to Russia, complaining that the Obama administration was 'trying to delegitimise the Trump administration as it goes into the White House'.

Someone else was busy denying the allegations too: Nigel Farage. 'Julian Assange … is absolutely clear that all the information he has got is not from Russian sources,' Farage said. So that was fine. Nigel also paid a visit to Assange in early March 2017. He was caught coming out of the red brick building behind Harrods, where Assange had been holed up so long, the day after WikiLeaks released another tranche of files detailing the CIA's counter-espionage operations.

When asked what he was doing, Farage said, 'I never discuss where I go or who I see.' It was quickly pointed out that this was odd, because just a few days earlier Nigel had tweeted a picture of himself at a table with Donald Trump and captioned it 'Dinner with the Donald'.

Odder still, Farage also told reporters he couldn't 'remember' anything about the meeting he'd just had in the embassy. Wags were also soon joking that Farage was not the first person to emerge from being alone in a room with Julian Assange with no memory of what just happened. But of course, there were other implications. The kind of implications that would naturally lead, at this crucial point in the screenplay, to the main characters removing their human masks, revealing their true lizard form and starting to laugh about all the human blood they were going to drink together.

In our world, however, we're stuck with Julian Assange, in a dark room, staring at a computer monitor, silently plotting, continually getting away with it.

STEVE BANNON

—

Date of birth: *27 November 1953*
In a nutshell: *Oh God, oh shit, we're all doomed*
Connected to: *Vladimir Putin, Donald Trump, Nigel Farage*

When Donald Trump appointed Steve Bannon as his chief counsellor and chief strategist, former Ku Klux Klan leader David Duke said it was 'excellent' news. Not everyone agreed. And it wasn't just the fear that Bannon was a 'white nationalist'.* Bannon seemed woefully under-qualified for the job. All he'd done was run the racist website Breitbart, work for Goldman Sachs for a few years and produce a series of weird films.

Judging by the chaos of Trump's early months in the presidency it would be easy to conclude that Bannon is to strategy what pins are to balloons and that he's every bit as incompetent as everyone suspected.

---

* Democratic House Speaker Nancy Pelosi was among those who gave him this label.

But there's a paradox here. Bannon seemed like an intellectual titan compared with Trump and most of the people around him precisely because he'd worked for a bank, produced whacky films and edited a website that ran articles containing regular punctuation and paragraphs longer than 140 characters. So it was also widely presumed he was the shadowy power behind Trump's gaudy golden throne. *Time* magazine even asked: 'Is Steve Bannon the Second Most Powerful Man in the World?'

He certainly seems to have had considerable impact on the international kindness and well-being quotient. Bannon helped draft Trump's aggressive inaugural address and was widely presumed to have been the brains (if that's the right word) behind Trump's early failed attempts to ban people from selected Muslim countries from entering the USA. When Bannon appeared at the Conservative Political Action Conference early in 2017, he also gave the most coherent overview of Trump's policy priorities we'd heard so far. These partly explained the chaos – since Bannon said he wanted to see the 'deconstruction of the administrative state'. In case that isn't worrying enough, he also said that all policy would be predicated on the kind of nationalism that animates the SNP and UKIP and has torn apart the UK. The USA, he explained, was not just an economic unit in a borderless world. It was 'a nation with a culture' and 'a reason for being'.

That idea becomes especially troubling when Bannon's theories about history, sex and race are factored in. Those videos Bannon made put forward a lot of unsettling ideas. In *Generation Zero*, as well as trying to suggest that hippies caused the 2008 financial crisis rather than market deregulation, Bannon outlines theories about crisis points in history. He says there are eighty-year cycles that lead to crashes, conflict and chaos. He says we're currently enjoying one of those periods of meltdown and involved in a fight for our lives. This fight for Bannon is mainly about crushing Islam.

Which partly explains that 'Muslim ban' on planes – and also why Breitbart ran so many articles suggesting that Muslims pose a rape threat to Western women* and became notorious for running head-lines like 'Political Correctness Protects Muslim Rape Culture'.

Other charming (and similarly unsubstantiated) topics on Breitbart have included: 'Trannies 49 Xs Higher HIV Rate', 'Birth Control Makes Women Unattractive and Crazy' and 'Bill Kristol: Republican Spoiler, Renegade Jew'.

Nice.

Bannon has always denied being an anti-Semite, but plenty of people have detected an unpleasant whiff about him – like one of his ex-wives who accused him of all kinds of ugly hatred during divorce proceed-ings in 2007. He's also tweeted an image of Hillary Clinton that included a Star of David on top of a pile of money. The producer of the sitcom *Seinfeld*, Peter Mehlman, also remarked in *The Guardian*: 'If he's not antisemitic, what do you have to do to be considered antisemitic? Shoot Woody Allen?'

But there was more to Breitbart than simple nastiness. One of its chief investors was Robert Mercer, a man who also helped UKIPs Brexit campaign, and funded Cambridge Analytica (on whose board Bannon sits), the company that famously took advantage of data on Facebook in order to profile users and target them with political messages. Breitbart also helped boost anti-Clinton material (some have suggested in concert with Russian bots that fed the stories around social media) whenever Trump was slumping in the polls during the 2016 election.

---

* A typical far-right idea. The Nazis also loved to roll it out about Jews and other races.

By this stage, Bannon is indeed sounding like a terrifying intellect – even if he's also one who believes, as he told *The Hollywood Reporter*, that 'darkness is good' and that Darth Vader had a good thing going when it comes to 'power'. But intelligence isn't everything. Peter Mehlman, who started sounding off about Bannon thanks to the revelation that Bannon made a fortune from investing early in *Seinfeld* – and still gets cash every time the beloved comedy is aired – also admitted that Bannon was 'smart' for buying those shares. But, he added, it 'doesn't make him any less miserable as a human being'.

DONALD TRUMP

—

Date of birth: *14 June 1946*

In a nutshell: *70-year-old toddler*

Connected to: *Vladimir Putin, Steve Bannon, Ayn Rand, Nigel Farage,*
Rex Tillerson

The trouble with writing about Donald Trump is that anything I say now will almost immediately become outdated. And I'm not talking about the lag between writing this book and getting it published. I'm talking about the time between starting one sentence and finishing the next. He is so unpredictable that for all I know even as I type these words he could be tweeting an announcement of World War III, a furious denunciation of all of his former allies, or just weird thoughts on the kinds of shoes he prefers women to wear. There's little point in going into detail about his ties to Putin and the Russians, his business failures, his debt restructurings that have seen creditors lose millions, his mysteriously absent tax returns, his fascist stigmatisation of Muslims, his attempts to lose medical protection for millions of Americans, his cancelling of meals on wheels for old folks while ensuring the US state spends far more money getting him down to

Florida to play golf every weekend, or about the bizarre lies and the alternative facts spread by his cabinet of lizards. Anything I set down now is likely to be almost immediately superseded by something far more revolting, revealing, frightening or despicable.

But luckily, I don't have to write anything anyway. The 45th President of the United States is more than capable of speaking for himself. Take it away Donald:

Nobody can do it like me.
Nobody has better toys than I do.
Nobody can do it like me. Honestly. Nobody is stronger than me.
There's nobody bigger or better at the military than I am.
Nobody's fighting for veterans like I'm fighting for veterans.
Nobody loves the Bible more than I do.
Nobody builds walls better than me.
There's nobody that's done so much for equality as I have.
Nobody would be tougher on ISIS than Donald Trump.
There's nobody more pro-Israel than I am.
Nobody knows more about trade than me.
There's nobody more conservative than me.
Nobody knows more about taxes than I do.
Nobody knows more about debt than I do.
Nobody knows the system better than me.
Nobody's ever had crowds like Donald Trump has had.
There's nobody that respects women more than I do.
Nobody knows politicians better than I do.
Nobody in the history of this country has ever known so much about infrastructure as Donald Trump.
Nobody knows the game better than I do.
There's nobody that understands the horror of nuclear better than me.

The president has also expanded on precisely what he understood about the 'horror' of 'nuclear':

> We had Hillary Clinton give Russia 20 per cent of the uranium in our country. You know what uranium is, right? It's this thing called nuclear weapons. And other things. Like lots of things are done with uranium. Including some bad things.

Naturally this claim about Hillary Clinton was untrue. On the subject of untruth, Trump has said:

> A few days ago, I called the fake news 'the enemy of the people', and they are. They are the enemy of the people. Because they have no sources. They just make them up where there are none.

In case you need clarification about fake news, he also once said:

> Well, the leaks are real. You're the one that wrote about them and reported them; I mean, the leaks are real. You know what they said, you saw it and the leaks are absolutely real. The news is fake because so much of the news is fake.

Talking of leaks, we better get this one* out of the way:

> I moved on her very heavily. In fact, I took her out furniture shopping.

> She wanted to get some furniture. I said, 'I'll show you where they have some nice furniture.'...

---

* No, not that one. At the time of writing, we still await the full story about the allegations that Putin is blackmailing Trump with a video of him enjoying a golden shower.

I moved on her like a bitch. But I couldn't get there. And she was married. Then all of a sudden I see her, she's now got the big phony tits and everything. She's totally changed her look ...

Yeah, that's her. With the gold. I better use some Tic Tacs just in case I start kissing her. You know, I'm automatically attracted to beautiful – I just start kissing them. It's like a magnet. Just kiss. I don't even wait. And when you're a star, they let you do it. You can do anything ...

Grab 'em by the pussy. You can do anything.

That notorious recording of Trump talking to Billy Bush from *Access Hollywood* isn't the only time Trump has waxed lecherous about women. On the *Howard Stern Show* he once described an ex-wife as 'nice tits, no brain'. And when the *New Yorker* writer Mark Singer asked Trump about his interior life and how he felt when he was alone, Trump replied: 'You really want to know what I consider good company? ... A total piece of ass.' And yes, Trump does have plenty to say about ass too. For instance: 'Would I approve waterboarding. You bet your ass. In a heartbeat. In a heartbeat. I would approve more than that.'

There are other things that Trump has approved of already. Speaking of his financial schemes, for instance, he once said: 'It's always good to do things nice and complicated so that nobody can figure it out.' And talking of his supporters, he declared: 'I love the poorly educated!' He also explained that if he saw people thinking about leaving during his rallies, he'd start saying: '"We will build a wall" – and they go nuts.' At one of those rallies in North Carolina, he told the crowd that he is 'maybe truthful to a fault'. So *The Huffington Post* went over the transcript of an hour-long speech he made – with ad breaks – in Wisconsin and found '71 separate incidents in which Trump made a claim that was inaccurate, misleading or deeply questionable'.

All of which rather makes you question Donald J. Trump's place in the world. But if you're feeling in any way superior, just remember what he told *Time* magazine:

> *Hey look, in the meantime, I guess, I can't be doing so badly, because I'm president, and you're not. You know. Say hello to everybody, OK?*

BENJAMIN FRANKLIN

—

Date of birth/death: *6 January 1705 – 17 April 1790*
In a nutshell: *Clever man who unwittingly enabled mumbo jumbo to conquer the world*
Connected to: *Donald Trump, L. Ron Hubbard*

In 1733, Benjamin Franklin published a book called *Poor Richard's Almanack* and set in motion a train that would eventually help chuff Donald Trump and his 'alternative facts' into world history.

Today Franklin is most famous as the enlightened brainbox who provided the intellectual backbone for the USA's independence struggle from Britain, who used kites to harness lightning and who invented bifocal glasses. But it's his early version of the go-get-'em self-help manual that initially made his name – and that made our world worse.

Among other things, *Poor Richard's Almanack* set out the blueprint for the American literary staple, the instruction manual for the attainment of wealth and happiness. Franklin peppered his Almanack with homely words of advice that encouraged Americans to work, work some more and then mistreat women. His famous phrases include such exhortations to labour and greed as 'Little strokes fell great oaks', 'Get what you can, and what you get hold' and 'Early to bed, early to rise, makes a man healthy, wealthy and wise.' He also told his readers 'Let thy maidservant be faithful, strong, and homely', 'Marry your son when you will, but your daughter when you can' and 'After three days men grow weary, of a wench, a guest, and weather rainy.'

Thankfully, not all his instructions have been remembered or followed. But the central lessons of Franklin's career as a writer remain with us. He helped pioneer the idea that all Americans could get rich if only they read the right books (and conversely, that if they didn't, they weren't helping themselves enough). He was also the first person to show that the only way to get rich from a get-rich book is to write one. He sold thousands of copies of his Almanack (and also very healthy numbers of other books with titles like *The Way to Wealth* and *Advice to Young Tradesmen*) and made a fortune.

These lessons were well learned by a man called Dale Carnegie. In 1936 he published another book about ways to wealth called *How to Win Friends and Influence People*. It has now sold over 16 million copies. Franklin's inspiration can also be seen in the many aphorisms Carnegie enjoyed using.* The book also contained many tips on 'handling people', how to win people over to 'your way of thinking' and how to 'change people' without upsetting them or arousing resentment. A cynic could suggest that it may as well have been called: how to take advantage of people, treat them like rungs on your ladder to success and tread on their faces as you ascend. But there is a kinder view. Carnegie at least encouraged his readers to listen, to smile and be genuinely interested in other people.

---

* He adored chapter titles like 'If You Want to Gather Honey, Don't Kick Over the Beehive'.

But soon the self-help train was running off the tracks. More and more books were published, and more and more of them encouraged their readers to be sociopaths. Chief among them was the work of a charismatic preacher called Norman Vincent Peale. He took Carnegie's model and used it to produce a book called *The Power of Positive Thinking*.

The Power of Positive Thinking was full of Carnegie- and Franklin-style advice, a typical idea being that if his readers were feeling defeated they should make a list, not of the things against them, but instead of those that were for them. But Peale took things further than his predecessors. His main method of overcoming defeat was to 'prayerise, visualise, actualise'. He told his readers to 'stamp indelibly' on their minds an image of themselves succeeding and to never permit it to fade. 'Attitudes', he urged, are more important than 'facts'. This idea, Peale said, is worth repeating 'until its truth grips you'.

In other words, if you think it's right it is right. If you visualise it strongly enough and believe it hard enough it becomes 'true'. But, of course, that's no kind of truth at all. That's an alternative fact. And so it is that Vincent Peale has helped shape our world.

If that's sounding far-fetched, well – everything is far-fetched nowadays. A reality TV star is the President of the USA. A reality TV star, incidentally, who was a close family friend of Norman Vincent Peale. Who had Peale officiate at his first wedding. Who had proponents of the Peale-influenced prosperity gospel* say prayers at his inauguration. Who also at his inauguration claimed that the sun was shining, when it wasn't. Who later said: 'God looked down and he said, "We're not going to let it rain on your speech."' Even though

---

* The belief that God grants health and wealth to those who do the right kind of believing.

rain was bouncing off his nose and the crowd in front of him was wearing plastic ponchos. A crowd, incidentally, which Trump kept maintaining was the biggest ever, even though all the evidence was against him. And also, a crowd full of people wearing hats bearing the legend 'Make America Great Again', a phrase that can itself be seen as a Peale-style visualisation. Not least because there's no other evidence that things are going to be great at all.

In short, the USA has a president who believes he can reshape reality just by thinking about it hard enough, and who thinks it's right to deny reality if it doesn't accord with his wishes, thanks to a bogus self-help theory descended from an almanac written in the eighteenth century. And if you're finding that thought frightening, well, a wise man once wrote, 'There are no gains without pains.' Or perhaps even more to the point: 'The Family of Fools is ancient.' It seems that Benjamin Franklin may still be worth listening to, after all.

L. RON HUBBARD

Date of birth/death: *13 March 1911 – 24 January 1986*

In a nutshell: *Narconon man*

Connected to: *Adolf Hitler, Benjamin Franklin*

'I have high hopes of smashing my name into history so violently that it will take a legendary form … That goal is the real goal as far as I am concerned.' So said L. Ron Hubbard in a letter to his first wife Margaret Grubb in 1938. He also told many people that he believed that the best way to make a fortune was to become the founder of a religion. And went on to prove himself spectacularly right by inventing Scientology.

Before he did, however, he tried out black magic. Around the end of World War II, Hubbard became involved with Aleister Crowley* and his disciple Jack Parsons† in their occult society. Along with Parsons, Hubbard tried to bring the goddess Babalon down to Earth in a ritual called 'Babalon Working'. Crowley wasn't impressed and wrote: 'I get frantic when I consider the idiocy of these louts.' Crowley also described Hubbard's relationship with Parsons as 'the ordinary confidence trick', a suspicion that was borne out when Hubbard ran off with Parsons' girlfriend Sara Northrup, along with most of his money. He then married Northrup before he divorced Grubb.

Poor Grubb. Hubbard's son, Ron Hubbard Jr, once told *Penthouse* magazine that he saw his father carrying out an abortion on her with a coat hanger. He further claimed that his father thought he was the Antichrist and compared him to Hitler for good measure. In the same interview, Hubbard Jr also revealed that Hubbard Sr had tried cocaine, amphetamine, peyote and barbiturates. In fact, he said, it would be shorter to list the drugs that the elder Hubbard hadn't sampled.

This latter revelation may surprise anyone who knows about Scientology. The church has long maintained a hard-line anti-drugs stance, and even run a programme called Narconon in schools, ostensibly dedicated to educating children about the dangers of narcotics.

Scientology watchers will be less surprised to learn that back in 2005, the State Superintendent of California urged all its educational

---

* The author of *The Diary of a Drug Fiend* and the black magick text *The Book of the Law*. During his lifetime he was known as 'the wickedest man alive'. His own mother called him: The 'Beast 666'.

† Also a pioneering rocket scientist. Go figure.

institutions to stop allowing the Narconon men and women into classrooms. The *San Francisco Chronicle* had reported that the children had been passed some rather odd information – like the idea that drug residues can be sweated out in saunas and that coloured ooze is produced when drugs exit the body. Furthermore, the pupils had also been told rather too much about the benefits of Scientology.

Those supposed benefits were first outlined in a book called *Dianetics* that Hubbard published in 1950, when he was a struggling science-fiction writer. *Dianetics* was a guide to a therapeutic technique that Hubbard said could cure all mental illnesses and psychosomatic illnesses – which is to say, illnesses caused by the mind. Since Hubbard claimed that nearly 70 per cent of seemingly physical illnesses were actually caused by the mind, this was a very healthy proportion of man's ills. He had hit upon a winning formula. Like many of the most effective self-help books, *Dianetics* simplified serious problems and offered big promises to its troubled readers.

Hubbard began to attract followers and money. He also began to attract the attention of the tax authorities, but successfully fended them off by claiming he had established a religion* and that his Dianetics procedures were a part of the Church's sacred liturgy rather than 'medical'.

These procedures involved a series of tests known as 'auditing' or 'clearing'. They are used to help eliminate the 'reactive mind' – the mind weakened by harmful experiences. These experiences are engraved in mental pictures called 'engrams', many of which have happened in the past lives of the subject's true self. The true self is known as the 'thetan'.

---

* Tax-exempt.

Yes, lots of jargon. But don't worry. There is an explanation.

Deep breath.

Seventy-five million years ago our planet Earth was part of a confederation of ninety planets under the leadership of Xenu, a ruthless tyrant. Xenu decided to cure an ongoing intergalactic overpopulation problem by paralysing the excess people, flying them to Earth in space planes, dropping them near volcanoes and dropping H-bombs on them. The souls of these unfortunate extra folk (the 'thetans') were then taken to cinemas and shown films for several days. The end result was that the souls hung around and now inhabit Earth's current residents and infect them with engrams. Which is to say, they infect us. These engrams have to be removed – and that's where Dianetics steps in, with its emphasis on auditing and clearing.

No one said the explanation would make sense. Until the advent of the internet and the release of documents about Xenu (handwritten by Hubbard himself), this strange story was also largely a secret. Only top-level Scientologists would be given the knowledge, after they had spent years in training – and also in giving money to the Church. One of Hubbard's big wheezes had been to claim that ever-higher levels of spiritual enlightenment could be obtained by repeated testing and spiritual auditing. Members of the Church could gradually climb the scale until they received awesome powers of awareness and mental control. This progression didn't come cheap, however.* The information about Xenu used to be one of the last things Scientologists learned – by which stage they had generally committed so much time and money that Hubbard must have reasoned that even a story as absurd as his Xenu myth wouldn't put them off.

---

* It still doesn't. Some estimates have put the cost to an average person of getting to the top of the ladder of Scientology at up to $500,000.

The continuing wealth and influence of the church Hubbard founded is testimony to the soundness of that gamble. Mind you, he still took no chances. He always kept a suitcase of money beside him so he would be able to do a runner whenever necessary. Towards the end of his life it appeared that the suitcase would be urgently needed. High-level defectors from the Church began accusing Hubbard of stealing millions of dollars. The American revenue service also began seeking an indictment for tax fraud. Hubbard died before the case could be prosecuted – but not before a California judge declared that the old man was 'a pathological liar'.*

---

* In a 1984 case in which the Scientologists sued one of Hubbard's biographical researchers.

JERRY FALWELL

—

Date of birth/death: 11 August 1933 – 15 May 2007
In a nutshell: *Famous for claiming he didn't sleep with his mum in an outhouse*
Connected to: *Ronald Reagan, George W. Bush, Donald Trump*

If posterity remembers Jerry Falwell, it will probably be as he appeared in *Hustler* magazine. He featured in a mock Campari ad, based on a long-running campaign for the drink where famous people would remember their 'first time'. *Hustler* had Falwell recalling that his memorable moment happened in an outhouse with his mother when 'drunk off our God-fearing asses on Campari'.

Falwell did not enjoy this portrayal. He sued the magazine's publisher Larry Flynt in a case that went all the way to the US Supreme Court in 1988. 'The First Amendment is not without limits,' said Falwell. He was wrong. Flynt won on freedom of speech grounds, with the court ruling that plaintiffs could not recover damages based on emotional distress suffered from parodies. So we have Falwell to thank for the fact that comedians on late night American TV can discuss politicians' gonads and golden showers whenever they like.

But that's about the only favour Falwell did for liberals. Otherwise, he worked tirelessly to stymie freedom and oppress the voiceless.

'The idea that religion and politics don't mix was invented by the Devil to keep Christians from running their own country,' Falwell claimed. He was a fundamentalist Christian preacher, convinced that there had once been a better time and that his mission was to help bring it back. This message that change is loss worked potently among conservatives and Southern voters convinced that their best days had passed and eager to make things great again. Great for themselves, anyway.

In the 1960s, Falwell featured pro-segregation politicians like George Wallace on his pioneering TV evangelism show *Old Time Gospel Hour*. Falwell, never one to spurn an opportunity to get on the wrong side of history, also campaigned hard against Martin Luther King. Once all-white public schools were declared illegal, Falwell established a line of private segregationist schools. And when Jimmy Carter's Democrat administration stripped these schools of their tax-exempt status in the late 1970s, Falwell really went on the warpath. The result was the foundation of an organisation called the Moral Majority in 1979. This was a group that reached four million members at its peak and claimed dedication to the promotion of traditional family life, fervent opposition to gun control, dislike of equality for women, refusal to accept homosexual rights and opposition to female choice on abortions.

The Moral Majority became one of the earliest supporters of Ronald Reagan's presidential bid in 1980 and, as Jimmy Carter explained it, 'that autumn a group headed by Jerry Falwell purchased $10 million in commercials on southern radio and TV to brand me as a traitor to the South and no longer a Christian'. It's been estimated that at least a fifth of Moral Majority supporters switched from Carter to Reagan. After the election, a triumphant Falwell announced that Reagan's success was directly because of the Moral Majority.

Reagan thanked Falwell by putting Moral Majority people in the Education Department. This was an interesting choice. Falwell had once proclaimed 'Textbooks are Soviet propaganda' and believed the Earth was created in seven days. No matter. The two men continued to work together. Falwell thanked Reagan in turn by helping to ensure his re-election in 1984, before eventually dissolving the Moral Majority in 1989, declaring: 'Our goal has been achieved ... The religious right is solidly in place and ... religious conservatives in America are now in for the duration.'

Jerry Falwell also worked hard to make sure he personally maintained a high profile. As well as campaigning for Reagan, he kept himself busy in the 1980s by opposing sanctions against the apartheid regime in South Africa and urging his followers to push for US reinvestment in the country.

During his long life he also took the time to insult other racial and religious groups. 'I think the Muslim faith teaches hate,' he said. He told *60 Minutes* viewers that Muhammad was 'a terrorist ... a violent man, a man of war'. And he told his followers that 'Jews can make more money accidentally than you can on purpose.' Jewish people, he also explained in his book *Listen, America!* were 'spiritually blind and desperately in need of their Messiah and Savior'. Just for good measure, he added in 1999 that the Antichrist would probably arrive within a decade and 'of course he'll be Jewish'.

Nor was he kind about homosexuals. 'I truly cannot imagine men with men, women with women, doing what they were not physically created to do,' he said. Curiously, though, he seems to have spent a lot of time thinking about man-love. He even wrote an article condemning Tinky Winky, a character from the children's TV programme *The Teletubbies* for being purple, carrying a handbag and thus 'role modeling the gay lifestyle'. It was, he explained, 'damaging to the moral lives of children'.

He also said: 'AIDS is not just God's punishment for homosexuals, it is God's punishment for the society that tolerates homosexuals.' 'God's punishment' was one of his big themes. After 9/11, he said: 'I really believe that the pagans, and the abortionists, and the feminists, and the gays and the lesbians who are actively trying to make that an alternative lifestyle, the ACLU, People for the American Way, all of them who have tried to secularize America, I point the finger in their face and say "You helped this happen."'

He thereby neatly mopped up plenty of the minority groups that he hadn't yet offended. During the Bush era he also kept his eye in when it came to undermining scientists, saying for instance: 'I believe that global warming is a myth. And so, therefore, I have no conscience problems at all and I'm going to buy a Suburban next time.'

Falwell loved Bush. He supported him right through his primaries and declared: 'I am such a strong admirer of George W. Bush that if he suggested eliminating the income tax or doubling it, I would vote yes on first blush.' Bush, in turn, frequently called Falwell and spoke to the preacher just days before his death in 2007. But Falwell's influence didn't end there. His schools still flourish, as does his religious higher education institution, Liberty University. Just as popular is that hankering for a once great America. On this subject, Falwell's son Jerry Jr has also carried on his father's good work. He was the first significant evangelical leader to endorse Trump in January 2016, before the Iowa caucus. Jerry Jr blamed the leak of the infamous 'grab 'em by the pussy' tape on 'establishment Republicans', saying it was 'timed' to disrupt the Trump campaign and that Trump 'apologized, he was contrite about it, he moved on to the issues, which is what the American people care about'.

In thanks, Trump put Falwell in charge of an educational task force to 'stop regulations' coming out of the education department. CNN reported that Falwell has been 'particularly interested' in curbing rules that required schools to investigate campus sexual assault. His daddy would have been delighted.

In 1994 Falwell gave $200,000 to an organisation called 'Citizens for Honest Government', which produced a film called *The Clinton Chronicles: An Investigation into the Alleged Criminal Activities of Bill Clinton*.

The film still crops up regularly on fake news sites, which often claim that those involved in making it have since been murdered or 'died under questionable circumstances'. It makes for surprising viewing, alleging, without evidence, that Clinton organised gun running and cocaine smuggling, and caused the deaths of dozens of journalists and other people who found out about his illegal activities and extramarital affairs. Jerry Falwell appears in the film interviewing a silhouetted reporter who claims to be afraid for his life and reels off a spiel of accusations against Clinton. This 'reporter' was later revealed to be Patrick Matrisciana, the president of Citizens for Honest Government and producer of the video.

JESUS CHRIST

—

Date of birth/death: *4 BC* – c. AD 30/33*

In a nutshell: *Naughty boy*

Connected to: *Jerry Falwell, George W. Bush, Tony Blair, Theresa May, Adolf Hitler*

Don't worry. There won't be any criticism of the historical Jesus here. Not least because there's little reliable evidence about his time on Earth. For all we can say, he was a stand-up guy. Sadly, we can't say the same thing about the other Jesus. The one we've all created. That Jesus is a real douche.

The trouble started a few decades after Jesus is supposed to have died, when people began composing books about his deeds, mashing together Old Testament prophecies to help convince people he was the Messiah and writing lots of stories about his vicious mean streak. Bible Jesus tells us that most people on Earth are sinners and will

---

* Historians generally say Jesus was born between four and seven years before the Year of Our Lord. I know. But then, none of the rest makes sense, really.

burn in hellfire. (He's really into hellfire.) He spreads the belief that sick or mentally ill people contain demons – and that to make them better, you have to cast out the demons. He demands repentance. He says that even fancying a woman is a lustful act and will get you in big trouble with the 'Guy in the Sky'. He gets angry. (He gets angry a lot.) He threatens that cities that don't accept his disciples will be blasted with fire from the air like Sodom and Gomorrah. He asks you to be a lickspittle. He also tells people that they shouldn't worry about washing their hands. Which is just bad advice. Silly Jesus.

There's also this:

> Think not that I am come to send peace on earth: I came not to send peace, but a sword. For I am come to set a man at variance against his father, and the daughter against her mother, and the daughter in law against her mother in law. And a man's foes shall be they of his own household. He that loveth father or mother more than me is not worthy of me: and he that loveth son or daughter more than me is not worthy of me. And he that taketh not his cross, and followeth after me, is not worthy of me.

Passages like that beauty have been used as an excuse for the spreading of death and destruction and misery for centuries.

Christ worship first became a weapon of state-sanctioned mass-murder in AD 312 when the emperor Constantine decided he wanted God on his side. According to his chronicler Eusebius, he had a vision of the symbol of Christ just before the Battle of the Milvian Bridge, which he used to inspire his troops. Also to justify the fact that after securing victory, he established the long-running Christian tradition of slaughtering his retreating foes.

Soon after that bloody victory, Constantine gathered committees of bishops at Nicaea to decree the most politically acceptable version of his new faith. In the process he created the notion of apostasy and outsiders. He also began 1,700 more years of confusion and bloodshed and bizarre behaviour in the name of poor old Jesus Christ, ranging from witch hunts, to Crusades, to invading Poland* via plenty of weird stuff about exorcism, getting scared about other people's sex lives and eating fish on Friday.

Even today Theresa May says Jesus is helping her find the way out of Europe. Not long ago Tony Blair claimed Jesus told him it was okay to invade Iraq. And that's before we get to the fact that he made Bob Dylan put out all those dreadful albums in the early 1980s. Before we get to Cliff Richard …

---

* Contrary to popular belief, Adolf Hitler liked Jesus and his sky-daddy. He even gave them props after he invaded Poland, saying: 'I can thank God at this moment that He has so wonderfully blessed us in our hard struggle for what is right, and beg Him that we and all other nations may find the right way, so that not only the German people but all Europe may once more be granted the blessing of peace.' Safe to say, that didn't work out too well.

IBN ABD AL-WAHHAB

—

Date of birth/death: *1703 – 22 June 1792*
In a nutshell: *Religious maniac*
Connected to: *George W. Bush, Osama bin Laden*

A few hundred years after people like John Calvin started frowning upon drink, Christmas and other healthy pleasures, a man called Ibn Abd al-Wahhab instigated his own laughless revolution in his small corner of the country now called Saudi Arabia. And just as the puritans saw their fellow Christians as corrupt, al-Wahhab loathed his Islamic co-religionists. He longed to get back to a purer, simpler time, based on strict interpretation of the Koran and the teachings of the immediate contemporaries of the prophet Mohammad. Like plenty of other people who have tried to turn back time, he made the future much worse.

Al-Wahhab's ideals were laid out in a book called *Kitab al-Tawhid*. He demanded conformity: that all Muslims must pledge allegiance to a single Muslim leader and belief system. He said that those who did not agree should be killed. Their belongings should be taken away.

Their wives and daughters should be violated. He considered most other Muslim sects to be apostate. He also had bad news for everyone else. Those who didn't worship Allah worshipped false idols and so were sorcerers and: 'The punishment for the sorcerers/magicians is that he be stuck with the sword.'

Once he had decided that the vast majority of the world's population deserved to die, al-Wahhab got busy. He started out small. He made an alliance with a local leader and began to make life unpleasant for his neighbours. He levelled a grave that locals liked visiting, since one of his big bug-bears was the worship of any kind of false idol. For the same reason, he cut down a popular grove of trees. Third, and most characteristically, he personally organised the stoning and murder of a woman he said had committed adultery. Such acts did not make him universally popular. Soon a bigger tribal chief was telling al-Wahhab's friend to get rid of the meddlesome preacher and al-Wahhab found himself in exile.

But his wanderings didn't last long. He managed to forge another alliance with a tribal leader called Muhammad bin Saud. Like Constantine before him, bin Saud realised that taking on a new form of religion would give him political advantages. Religion provided his armies with new ideological ammunition, as well as a salve for his own conscience (assuming he had one.) Bin Saud was much given to raiding and stealing other territories – and now he could claim he was doing it in the name of spiritual reform. Together with al-Wahhab, bin Saud also reintroduced the idea of martyrdom in the name of jihad, telling those who died in battle they would gain immediate entry into paradise and a reception committee of willing virgins.

The newly motivated armies of Saud and Wahhab conquered most of present-day Saudi Arabia. And they didn't do it the nice way. In 1801, for instance, Saud carried out a massacre at Karbala, killing around

5,000 people, according to estimates at the time. A contemporary wrote: 'We took Karbala and slaughtered and took its people (as slaves), then praise be to Allah, Lord of the Worlds, and we do not apologise for that and say: "And to the unbelievers: the same treatment."'

By this time al-Wahhab himself had died, but his family remained close to Saud, forging bonds that helped ensure the alliance between the two houses has remained strong to this day. Until the twentieth century their strict religious beliefs were largely confined to their home country (and then often only small parts of it, as their fortunes ebbed and flowed). But with the arrival of petrochemical dollars the Saudi state began to proselytise. It spends billions of dollars each year on schools and mosques and educational resources around the world. In 2007, it was estimated that literature published and distributed by agencies linked to Saudi Arabia was in a quarter of the UK's mosques. A typical passage urged that homosexuals should be thrown from the top of tall buildings (and then also stoned on the ground, just in case).

On the subject of tall buildings, it was followers of al-Wahabb who carried out the outrage of 11 September 2001. The 7/7 suicide bombers in London, Mohammad Sidique Khan and Shehzad Tanweer, were Salafis. So too was Richard Reid, the daft lad who tried to smuggle a bomb onto an aeroplane in his shoe. The Islamic State is also an offshoot of Wahhabism – even if not one strictly condoned by the Saudi regime.

Of course, al-Wahhab is not the only source of Islamic terror. Many sects of Al Qaeda have their origins in the Muslim Brotherhood in Egypt. The Taliban are Deobandis, a revivalist group formed as a reaction to colonialism in Asia. Nor are all Wahhabi believers terrorists – or all Salafists believers in al-Wahhab's teachings. The vast majority are not violent. But this is a creed with cruelty written into its DNA. Al-Wahhab has made a great many young men feel they have a licence to rape, murder and impose their hatred on everyone else. He was a dickhead.

OSAMA BIN LADEN

—

Date of birth/death: *10 March 1957 – 2 May 2011*
In a nutshell: *Pioneering YouTube bore and mass-murderer*
Connected to: *George W. Bush, Ibn Abd al-Wahhab*

Osama bin Laden's crimes against innocent people would mark him out as a hateful extremist in any age. But there's also plenty about him that marks him out as just an average Joe.

As the over-entitled son of a rich and powerful family, who believed he had a direct phone line to his god, Osama wasn't so different from his arch-enemy George W. Bush. Meanwhile, as a man who liked nothing better than making crappy home videos that mainly just featured static shots of his own face talking angrily about all the things that were annoying him that day, he wasn't half so different to most of the world's population.

Bin Laden posed as an old-school medievalist, given to hanging out in caves in tribal outfits, far-removed from decent shaving tackle and quoting (at tedious length) from ancient books. But one of his most lasting legacies is in the world of high-tech communication. He was a proto-vlogger. He pioneered the broadcast of tacky home videos. He was one of the first to attract unaccountable millions of impressionable teen viewers to his online channel. Teens who hung on his every word – even though they were transparently nonsense. You could say bin Laden has as much in common with wannabe-Zoellas as he does with his religious heroes. Even his habit of cradling military hardware while he's on camera feels like a dark foreshadowing of later video bloggers' love of displaying their bling.

On the subject of materialism, meanwhile, bin Laden preached an anti-capitalist, anti-American, anti-commercial austerity, but of course when he was finally found in his million-dollar compound in Abbottabad he and his wives (yes, plural, all of them much younger than him) had fridges full of Coca-Cola and Pepsi. Their computer hard drives bulged with porn. In the end, he was as much a part of the world he wanted to destroy as anyone else. And while his murderous cruelty may have been extraordinary, his vanity and hypocrisy are all too familiar. As is his silliness.

GEORGE W. BUSH

Date of birth: 6 July 1946

In a nutshell: *Everything he touched has gone wrong. He's even stopped winning at being the worst president ever.*

Connected to: *Milton Friedman, Osama bin Laden, Tony Blair, Jerry Falwell*

'Compared to Donald Trump, George W. Bush looks like a paragon of statesmanship,' said Francis Fukuyama in 2015.

Fukuyama was also the man who in 1989 declared the 'end of history', when we would see the 'universalisation of Western liberal democracy as the final form of human government'. Which turned out to be a prediction on a par with the bank manager who famously turned down a loan to Henry Ford because 'the horse is here to stay.'

We might want to take Fukuyama's words with a pinch of salt. But it's easy to see why Bush suddenly seems preferable to the Mango Mussolini. There's no avoiding the contrast between him quietly working on his watercolours and the furious tweeting of the current president. And when Bush started saying he didn't like the 'racism' and 'name-calling' of the Trump leadership and also reminding us that the media was 'indispensable to democracy', it became ever more easy to feel sentimental about good old Dubya. Plus, Bush still has that gentle twinkle in his eye, that smile never far from his face, and his folksy Texan accent. He always looks like a guy you'd enjoy sharing a few drinks with in your local pub. But then again, I enjoy sharing a few drinks with my mate Will – but I'm damned if I'd want him anywhere near the nuclear button, let alone trying to deal with the fallout of September 11.

And tragically, Bush was there. Elements of Bush's response to that nightmare have been praised in the light of Trump's attacks on Muslims. George W. once made a reasonable speech pointing out that Islam is a religion of peace and reassuring American Muslims that he was not about to round them all up. That now seems relatively benign. Although, he did actually round up over 1,000 Muslims and detain them without trial. And also invade Iraq on the basis of a dodgy dossier of evidence about weapons of mass destruction. And so kill over 100,000 Muslim civilians, many of them women and children, not to mention thousands of US servicemen.

In the process of trumping up* all that fake material, Bush's administration also managed to convince a majority of Americans that Saddam Hussein was responsible for 9/11 and that Al Qaeda came from Iraq. Which they didn't. ISIS did though. Later on. And largely because Bush created such chaos and such a huge power vacuum there.

This messed-up aftermath of the Iraq war and the collapse of Iraqi state structures is generally attributed to the Bush administration's poor planning – and while there's truth in that, it's also worth point-

---

* Sorry.

ing out that the collapse of state structures was partly deliberate. The shock treatment would enable the new regime to carry out an experiment in Milton Friedman's economic theories. The big idea was to start from scratch with private companies running everything instead of state bodies running everything and so let the good old discipline of the markets create a boom that would soon have all the local citizens singing the praises of American-style democracy and eating in McDonald's. Just like all other attempts to impose Friedman's theories, it didn't work. Things got much worse. The country fell apart. And the only certainty became the fact that the US and their allies were behaving dreadfully, torturing people at prisons like Abu Ghraib, and shooting civilians from helicopters. All they succeeded in doing was creating the perfect breeding ground for ISIS.

Bush's domestic legacy is also atrocious. Possibly his most enduring contribution to ruining everything will be his decision to withdraw from the Kyoto Protocol and his failure to tackle the global warming crisis. He also taught Trump most of what he knows about staffing environmental posts with men (always men) with industrial ties to the very polluters they are supposed to regulate.

Elsewhere, Bush masterminded an economic policy that saw huge tax cuts for the rich, while most other households grew poorer, and saw a 100 per cent increase in national debt. His administration's determined failure to properly regulate markets helped bring on the 2007/8 market crash and the great recession. In the penultimate November of his presidency, 500,000 jobs disappeared. By the end of 2008, the economy had lost 2.6 million jobs.

Meanwhile, not-so-cuddly George smeared political opponents, prohibited same-sex marriage and chose Martin Luther King's birthday to announce his opposition to affirmative action. He might not be as bad as Trump. But not being as bad as the Donald is not a virtue. It's just the default position. Tony Blair isn't as bad as Donald

Trump either. Nor was your school bully. Nor was Shakespeare's Iago. Losing control of your bowels on a first date is not as bad as Donald Trump. And George W. Bush was still a war criminal, a murderer and the father of the recession that got us into this mess in the first place.

Bushisms

- 'I know the human being and fish can coexist peacefully.'
- 'There's an old saying in Tennessee – I know it's in Texas, probably in Tennessee – that says, "Fool me once, shame on … shame on you. Fool me – you can't get fooled again."'
- 'I'm the commander, see. I don't need to explain – I do not need to explain why I say things. That's the interesting thing about being the president. Maybe somebody needs to explain to me why they say something, but I don't feel like I owe anybody an explanation.'
- 'Rarely is the question asked: Is our children learning?'
- 'I just want you to know that, when we talk about war, we're really talking about peace.'

TONY BLAIR

—

Date of birth: *6 May 1953*
In a nutshell: *Things only got worse*
Connected to: *George W. Bush, Osama bin Laden*

Since the UK Brexit referendum, Tony Blair has been arguing passionately with Theresa May's government. He sees them bringing his country into danger and disgrace. He knows they are following a senseless agenda in the face of all reason. He despairs as they disregard empirical evidence, bend the truth and manipulate the right-wing media. He cringes to see them playing on popular prejudice, and he is appalled by their whiffy miasma of vendetta and racism. He is furious. He knows no one in power is listening to him. He is all too aware that he is on the right side of history. He watches aghast and disenfranchised as this terrible juggernaut rolls on into an ever-bleaker future.

So now he knows how it damn well feels.

Now at last he is experiencing the outrage his country felt as he dragged it into the Iraq war in 2003: spreading lies and disinformation all the way, spouting nonsense about weapons of mass destruction, sucking up to a dangerous and vengeful American president, alienating our friends around the world, refusing to hear anyone who asked him to think properly about the consequences.

And those consequences were just as everyone warned. He caused unnecessary deaths and blighted lives. He threw a country into chaos. He encouraged uncontrollable extremists. He helped inflict a tragedy, and this will be his most enduring legacy.

But that's not the only way he failed us. When Tony Blair was elected on a wave of optimism in 1997, promising that 'things can only get better', he was given a huge mandate for change. But instead he just gave us more of the same. Sharply rising inequality. Spiralling house prices. Ever more irresponsible bankers.

Okay, he did some good tinkering around the edges. With hindsight the New Labour years can even seem like a golden age of prosperity and tolerance and social progress. But they were also a time of grinding frustration and disappointment. Not to mention irritation. Because Tony Blair was also annoying. He abused the English language. He always said, 'What I want to say to you is this', before saying next to nothing. He talked in participles. He was forever 'changing' the way we do things, 'making' life better, 'forward-looking', 'adding' value, 'listening carefully', 'warning' that Saddam was 'developing' weapons of mass destruction. He was always crapping on. He told us he would find us a 'third way'. But he didn't ever truly explain what that was. Nor did he tell us what the second way had been, or the first.

All we knew is that things were getting worse and that he wasn't listening to us. Primarily, because he was listening to a guy in the sky.

He might have had doubts about standing before the international court of justice, but Tony found he was easily able to justify his actions to himself because of his religious faith. He said he prayed to God before invading Iraq – and God, apparently, told him to go for it. 'In the end, there is a judgement that, I think if you have faith about these things, you realise that judgement is made by other people … and if you believe in God, it's made by God as well,' said Tony. So that's cool.

On the subject of religion, we are still to fully reap one of the most poisonous harvests from Tony Blair's time in office: his decision to increase the number of faith schools in the UK – and so allow our communities to be split along religious lines. Many of these schools have since been found to teach fundamentalisms of all kinds. And even in Blair's era, the dangers were clear. As usual, he blithely ignored them. When it was discovered that a school in Gateshead was teaching children that God created the world 6,000 years ago, an MP called Jenny Tonge asked the prime minister if he was 'happy to allow the teaching of creationism alongside Darwin's theory of evolution in state schools'. Blair told Tonge that he was 'very happy'. The fruitcakes in Gateshead were doing a fine job and getting very good results. A 'more diverse school system' was just what we needed, he said. A few days later he also went and lectured the Royal Society about the importance of 'proper science' and warned against a retreat into 'the culture of unreason'.

And it was because of such hypocrisy that the British people became ever more angry and distrustful. Wasn't it 'experts' that Tony Blair wheeled out to tell us about those WMDs? Mightn't we just as well vote for an outsider like Corbyn since all the other politicians have been just the same? Can we really believe the government's warnings about the dangers of leaving the EU? He started it. Even as he imposed his religion on us, Tony Blair made sure everyone else in the UK lost faith in everything.

JEREMY CORBYN

Date of birth: *26 May 1949*

In a nutshell: *The best thing that has ever happened to the Tory party*

Connected to: *Theresa May, Tony Blair, David Cameron, Vladimir Putin*

Shortly after nominating Jeremy Corbyn for the leadership of the Labour party the MP Margaret Beckett realised her mistake. 'I was a moron,' she said. 'At no point did I intend to vote for Jeremy myself – nor do I advise anyone else to do it.'

So far, the British public has taken this last bit of advice to heart. Corbyn's party has crashed in the polls. He hasn't connected with voters. They have just seen someone looking perpetually annoyed to have been dragged away from his vegetable patch. Someone, in fact, who is forever dodging off to be among his fruit and veg. Someone who was too busy making jam during one of the biggest scandals of his leadership to make any comments to the press. Someone who also sloped off to his allotment association's annual get together while most of his cabinet were busy resigning following the Brexit vote. This last absence should have come as no surprise. 'I always make time for my allotment,' he once told the *Independent*. 'You like a dry summer because the weeds don't grow. You water what you need to water and the weeds can sod off.'

That's about as close to a coherent political philosophy as we've come to expect from this most gnomic and gnomefaced of leaders. There are plenty of things he's against. But he's rather vaguer about what he's for. One day he supports Scottish independence, the next he's against. One day he's in favour of freedom of movement, the next not so much. One day he's in favour of wage caps ... You get the picture. When Corbyn stood on a platform of radical change, few knew that the thing he'd be changing most often would be his own mind.

But political savants at least might have predicted that like most 'change' candidates, Corbyn would quickly show that he was actually just like all the rest. Okay. Not quite like the other politicians. He was far worse at doing his job. Especially when it came to talking to the press. That jam story emerged following Corbyn's bodged attempts to score points against a privatised railway company. He was filmed ostentatiously sitting on the floor of a Virgin train, declaring, 'Today this train is completely ram-packed,' and calling for nationalisation. The only trouble was that CCTV images were quickly released showing that the train had had dozens of empty seats and that Corbyn had walked past them all before plonking himself down on the floor to make his film.

More seriously, Corbyn has repeatedly failed to crack down on anti-Semitism in the Labour Party – or even to investigate it properly. When he was forced to commission a report into the problem, he appointed the former leader of the Liberty pressure group Shami Chakrabarti to head it up. To no one's surprise, she discovered that the Labour Party wasn't overrun by racist creeps. Also to no one's surprise, a few weeks later Corbyn appointed her to the House of Lords.

Such glorious leadership has nearly destroyed the political party that created the NHS. Labour has fallen to historic lows in the polls. In the Copeland by-election in early 2017, Labour even lost a seat that had been in its hands since 1935. It also became the first opposition party to lose a parliamentary seat to the government in a by-election in more than thirty-five years.

'Opposition party' is now only a technical term, though. Because if Corbyn's Labour is notable for anything, it's for entirely failing to oppose the government. Corbyn's obedience to the government line is bitterly ironic. He was notorious for furiously opposing just about everything the government tried to do when the Labour Party was in power under Tony Blair and Gordon Brown.* He voted against his party whip 428 times – more votes against Labour than David Cameron notched up. But following the EU referendum, arguably the biggest crisis since World War II, Corbyn marched his MPs through the lobbies directly behind the prime minister. The quondam rebel imposed a three-line whip stating MPs must support Theresa May's Brexit Bill without amendments, safeguards on staying in the Single Market or protections for EU citizens. Once the bill had safely passed and our fate was sealed, he tweeted 'the real fight starts now'. Just to be sure he wasn't making sense, he also went and told the Labour Party in the House of Lords to rubber-stamp the bill too. A few weeks later, he also scheduled a protest outside Parliament calling for the government to guarantee the legal status of EU citizens in the UK.† In other words, a demo against the consequences of a vote he whipped his MPs to support. Don't worry. My brain hurts too.

* Other than that, his biggest contribution was being a member of the All-Party Parliamentary Group for Cheese.

† In the event, Corbyn dodged the demo, because fewer than 100 people turned up.

Conspiracy theorists see the confirmation of their worst fears in this lack of effective opposition. Corbyn stated he was pro-Remain during the Referendum, but plenty thought otherwise. His endorsements of the EU were never better than lukewarm. He worked less hard on the campaign trail than he ever did in his leadership bids – and he even took a mini-break at a crucial point in the run-up to the vote. He'd also consistently voted against the EU in Parliament in the past – and friends like Tariq Ali kept on saying that 'Jeremy is completely opposed to the EU.'

Especially paranoid conspiracy theorists could also have a field day linking Corbyn's support for Brexit to his frequent tendency to land on the same side of important arguments as one Vladimir Putin. Especially since Corbyn's Executive Director of Strategy is Seumas Milne, a man who has previously chaired events featuring the Russian leader at Putin's notorious annual propaganda summit in Sochi.*

But anyone who's seen Corbyn in action will be more inclined to take a softer line. His destruction of Labour as an electoral force, his failure to hold the government to account and his landing on the wrong side of history in the Parliamentary Brexit votes are clearly all just symptoms of his incompetence. The sooner he goes back to his allotment, the better off we'll all be.

---

* The cadaverous Director of Strategy, known unfondly as the Thin Controller, has also stated that Putin's invasion of the Crimea and military action in Ukraine were 'defensive'.

DAVID CAMERON

Date of birth: *9 October 1966*

In a nutshell: *Pig-fucker*

Connected to: *Theresa May, Jeremy Corbyn, Boris Johnson*

In one of his first major foreign affairs speeches as prime minister in 2010, David Cameron announced that under his leadership no one would see Britain 'shuffling apologetically off the world stage'.

Stop laughing.

In fact, you could even argue that this was one of the few promises that Cameron bothered to keep. If his rule did anything, it made sure that everyone, everywhere would start talking about Britain again.

The first big thing he did to raise our international profile was to become the subject of an astonishing rumour. *Call Me Dave*, a book about Cameron written by the journalist Isabel Oakeshott and Tory party donor Lord Ashcroft, told a surprising story. A Tory

MP* who went to Oxford University with the erstwhile prime minister claimed he saw him 'put a private part of his anatomy' into a dead pig's mouth. Soon jokes about going the whole hog were spreading North and South, East and West. Few people may care about the UK's place in the world any more – but at least a great many people know we once had a prime minister who may just have pounded a porker.

The second thing Cameron did to make everyone sit up and listen was to accidentally cause us to leave the world's most successful trading and peace project. The man who said he wanted to be prime minister 'because I think I'd be rather good at it' failed to convince the British people that leaving the European Union was a bad idea, and so made them the world's greatest laughing stock.†

But even though Cameron's disasters astonished the world – they were rather less surprising for everyone back in Britain. We'd had six years of him by then, and knew what he was like.

We'd also watched as Cameron broke promise after promise. 'Vote blue, go green,' he said, before tearing up environmental legislation, scrapping subsidies for alternative energy and allowing British cities to develop air pollution levels that have occasionally surpassed those of Beijing. There will be 'no top-down reorganisation of the NHS', he said, before his government organised the biggest restructuring in the service's history and brought it to the brink of ruin. 'We're all in this together,' he said – and then his government cut the top rate of taxes for the highest earners, while trying to impose VAT on pies and tearing apart the poor and needy with the casual cruelty and crowing relish that Cameron's red-suited chums show when they throw foxes to their hounds.

---

* Alas, the source remains anonymous.

† At least until Trump came along, anyway.

If it weren't for the EU catastrophe, Cameron's legacy would be food-banks and putting more people in the UK into poverty than at any time since the war. Oh, and perhaps the destruction of the Liberal Democrat political party. Because if you think Cameron was bad to the pig, you should see what he did to Nick Clegg. Cameron destroyed his Deputy Prime Minister and coalition government partner. Within twelve months of taking government, Cameron had pushed through a huge rise in student tuition fees, and so ensured that Clegg was seen to have betrayed his biggest campaign promise and faced electoral oblivion. Cameron subsequently laid just about every other unpopular policy at the poor old Lib Dems' door too.

But there is no getting around the fact that Cameron himself is responsible for Brexit. Almost as soon as he took over the Tory party, he had asked them to stop 'banging on about Europe'. There followed a decade of obsessive back and forth, made worse as Cameron ensured himself a weak-bargaining position on the continent by persistently alienating potential allies (one of his very first moves was to annoy Angela Merkel by pulling out of the European People's Party alliance) and allowing ministers like his incompetent Home Secretary Theresa May to blame their own shortfallings on EU policies.

Worst of all, he caved into pressure. 'He's so busy wondering how to get through the next few weeks that he could endanger Britain's international position for the next few decades,' said Nick Clegg. According to government minister David Laws' book *Coalition*, Clegg also pointed out the dangers of a poorly planned referendum in 2012. 'You may be right,' said Cameron. 'But what else can I do? My backbenchers are unbelievably Eurosceptic and UKIP are breathing down my neck.'

And that, in short, is why we're leaving the European Union. Because David Cameron couldn't manage his own party and was scared of Nigel Farage's angry-pensioner army. But even losing the referendum wasn't his final infamy. Before scuttling off to a life of handsomely rewarded speech-making and kitchen suppers with his posh friends in the Cotswolds, Cameron had a bit more cronyism to get through. Having already recommended a 24 per cent pay rise for his special advisers (when for years under his government public sector pay rises had been capped at 1 per cent), he gave them further generous redundancies when he left. He also put a large number of them on his departing honours list, along with numerous other buddies and Tory donors. He even gave an OBE to his wife's stylist.

And then he shuffled off into history, a live microphone catching him humming quietly to himself as he left Downing Street. Who knows what he was thinking? It's probably too much to hope that he recalled that 2010 speech when he also described Britain's 'strong and active' membership of the European Union as one of its greatest strengths. Back then Cameron said proudly: 'In terms of our role in the world, the truth is that many other countries would envy the cards we hold.' They don't any more, thanks to him.

LYNTON CROSBY

Date of birth: *23 August 1956*
In a nutshell: *Master of electoral dark arts*
Connected to: *David Cameron, Boris Johnson*

In 2005, when the Australian Lynton Crosby first became the UK Tory party election strategist, his campaign was dismissed as crude, divisive and unpleasant. 'Are you thinking what we're thinking?' asked Tory posters. Most people at the time said 'no'. Because back in that more innocent time, slogans like 'It's not racist to impose limits on immigration' felt, well, racist.

The party also ran posters asking: 'How would you feel if a bloke on early release attacked your daughter?' Newspapers at the time described these as an appeal to the 'lowest common denominator'. Australians who had seen Crosby in operation at home also had a warning for us. 'They will play to the basest of opinions in the coming weeks,' Bob Hogg, former campaigner for the Australian Labor Party told the *Guardian*. 'There's a dark underside to any human being and they pander to people's fears.'

But what Hogg knew – and British readers didn't fully realise in 2005 – was that Crosby's tactics worked. In Australia he had already overseen four successful election campaigns for the right-wing Liberal Party leader John Howard. His tactics had been highly controversial. Most notoriously, in 2001, Howard had accused asylum seekers of trying to blackmail their way into Australia by throwing children overboard from their refugee ship. The accusation was entirely untrue, but it did the job, helping to ensure Howard's anti-immigration ticket won the race. Such tactics also helped ensure that Australian political discourse moved ever further to the right.

Which brings us back to Britain. The Tories lost in 2005 – but Crosby subsequently helped Boris Johnson win two mayoral elections in London. By 2013, when he was signed up to help run David Cameron's 2015 election campaign, Conservative MPs were speaking admiringly of the very tactics that had once won Crosby opprobrium. 'There is only one type of politics Lynton Crosby understands,' said one Tory. 'He gets the vote out by really going for the lowest common denominator.'

Crosby didn't major on immigration in that 2015 election. Partly thanks to Crosby's earlier campaigns, the atmosphere had changed in the UK so much that he thought the issue was best left to the even more right-wing party UKIP. Crosby focused instead on ruthlessly targeting marginal seats, snatching votes from the Tories' Lib Dem coalition allies, and duffing up the Labour party leader Ed Miliband. Whenever things were going well for Labour, the Tories would say something horrible about poor old Ed. Ten days into the campaign, for instance, the defence minister Michael Fallon played on two of middle-England's biggest fears by saying that Miliband would scrap the Trident nuclear deterrent so he could strike an electoral deal with the hated Scottish National Party. And he didn't mince his words: 'Miliband stabbed his own brother in the back to become Labour leader,' he said, referring to the fact that Ed had taken his elder brother on in order to take over the party. 'Now he is willing to stab the United Kingdom in the back to become prime minister.'

Ouch. And don't let the 2015 campaign make you think Crosby had softened up when it came to racial politics. Afterwards, he managed the Tory MP Zac Goldsmith's* campaign to be London Mayor, and it was the most divisive and unpleasant in the capital's history. One of the dark arts Crosby was known for employing was the dog whistle. Which is to say, a message (often relating to immigration) that some people will react to and most people won't notice. But in the 2016 election, the Labour MP Yvette Cooper said that whistle turned into a 'racist scream'. Sadiq Khan, Goldsmith's Muslim opponent, was attacked as a 'radical', and accused of 'providing cover to extremists'. Meanwhile targeted leaflets were sent to Indian, Tamil and Sikh Londoners, claiming that Khan would not 'stand up' for them.

All that is ugly enough. So too is the fact that the man newspapers call 'the supreme master of the dark arts' has spent many lucrative years as a lobbyist for tobacco companies. But possibly his most malign influence on modern politics is his pioneering and mastery of a strategy known as the 'dead cat'. This idea was explained by Boris Johnson in an article about his Australian friend in 2013. He said that Crosby told him that if people are talking about the qualities of your opponents, or problems in your campaign, or things you've done wrong, you slap a dead cat on the table. People might be upset. They might even be disgusted. But it doesn't matter. The important thing is that everyone will shout: 'Jeez, mate, there's a dead cat on the table!' In other words, they'll all be talking the thing you want them to talk about – instead of the issue that's been causing you grief.

* Yes, this was the son of James Goldsmith.

The attacks on Ed Miliband's relationship with his brother were dead cats. So too was the refugee ship in Australia. Political campaigns around the world have watched and learned from Crosby. When it became clear that the Leave campaign in the UK Brexit referendum were losing the economic arguments they sent a big red bus around the country with a fantasy figure about contributions to the NHS painted on the side. And then there's Donald Trump. It's perfectly possible that his tweets and bizarre statements are just a function of his general oddness. But it's also possible that he's forever tweeting about Arnold Schwarzenegger's ratings on *The Apprentice* and FAKE NEWS and Obama-instigated wire taps to mess with our heads. Maybe – and this is the really frightening thought – it's all part of a plan. A plan he thought up thanks to Lynton Crosby …

KIM KARDASHIAN WEST

Date of birth: *21 October 1980*
In a nutshell: *Famous*
Connected to: *Lynton Crosby*

Lynton Crosby may have weaponised the 'dead cat strategy', and the idea that you should divert your opponents into talking about a subject you've raised by slapping a mortified moggy on the table, but distraction as a political tactic has been around for a long time. It's been with us at least since the days when Caligula told Roman senators that he was going to have his horse Incitatus made into a consul.

In those days too, they understood the importance of giving the people something to think about other than how awful their lives were. Today, this form of distraction is personified by Kim Kardashian. She is the entire world's dead cat. The richest 1 per cent of the population may be hoovering up ever more of the world's wealth, our politicians may be growing ever more hateful, global warming might be … but hey! Look over there! Kim Kardashian's got her bum out and taken a picture!

She is our soma, our people's opium, our bread and circuses all rolled into one – but with less of the wholesome fun of boshing drugs and watching punters get torn apart by lions.

If ever we want to talk about people who are famous just for being famous, we have to talk about Kim Kardashian first. She has taken things to a new level. She is famous for being famous just for being famous. And she's probably famous for all of that too. And there's something worrying about her rise to fame-fame-fame. Or rather, there's something worrying about the way there's nothing about it. She gets millions of pounds, but what has she done? What creative act has she brought to the world apart from herself? This is someone who first became famous* because she was friends with the rich reality TV star Paris Hilton – and who then went on to become even more famous† for becoming the star of a reality TV programme all about her own life and her family. She is someone who lent her name to a computer game – Kim Kardashian: Hollywood – where the main aim is to gain 'fans' by doing things like going on dates, and appearing at clubs. Someone whose biggest contribution to culture so far is a book of photos she took of herself called *Selfish*.

And the message that such self-promotion gives to the millions of people is that to be successful you don't have to do anything, you just have to be. Be yourself. All you need is you.

But there's a catch. Because *you* cannot be Kim Kardashian.

First, as she keeps reminding us all in her blingtastic social media feeds, she is much richer than us. She encourages the idea that conspicuous consumption is a good thing – but consumes more than

---

* For being famous for being famous.

† You know the drill.

we will ever be able to. The rings she wears are worth millions of pounds. Her houses are in exclusive neighbourhoods. Her cars alone are worth more than most of us will ever earn in our entire lives.

Second, she is more sculpted, gym-toned, calorie-counted, manicured, preened, dressed-up than most mortals can ever be. She presents an unobtainable ideal of beauty and does it again and again, day in day out, in countless social media reminders.

So there it is. We're trapped in a dilemma. Kim Kardashian both tells us that all you need to do to reach the pinnacle of our society is to be you – but also that if you're anything like most people, *you* are going to fail. But don't think about that too hard! Look! She's tweeting again! And this time it's serious. 'I never thought I would ever say this,' says this philosopher of our times, 'but I'm wearing flats today …'

CHRIS MARTIN

—

Date of birth: *2 March 1977*
In a nutshell: *Probably quite a nice man. But that's also part of his problem.*
Connected to: *The stars*

Old hippies used to like to claim that music died at the Altamont Speedway on 6 December 1969. When Hells Angels started pummel-ling the flower children at the Rolling Stones' infamous free concert, they said the rock and roll dream was over.

But old hippies talk a lot of nonsense. If anything, rock and roll took a more urgent turn after Altamont. Even the Rolling Stones had at least half a dozen terrifyingly good, not to mention down and dirty, albums still to come. Still to come too was Johnny Rotten spitting out home truths about the British Queen. Bruce Springsteen would tear into the Reagan administration. Public Enemy would rip up white America. The Happy Mondays and the rave generation would scare the living heck out of their parents all over again at the end of the 1980s. And Rage Against the Machine at least tried to wake us up in the 1990s ...

So rock and roll made it into the new millennium. It only died on 1 March 2000 when Coldplay released their globe-subduing single 'Yellow'. It was at this point that nothing anyone could do with a guitar mattered any more. All of rock and roll history had been wrapped up into a bland and vaguely wholesome sludge that wasn't going to upset or even excite anyone. Music just became background noise. It became something you could pipe into Starbucks with no fear of waking up anyone in the queue before they got their coffee. It became vacant and vague. Even Chris Martin himself has admitted he doesn't really know what the song means. And the worst thing is that 'Yellow' … isn't that bad. Nor all the other million-selling songs Coldplay have pumped out since. You can't even get annoyed. Their music is melodic and gentle and completely harmless. Except for the fact that there's something about those Vaseline thick guitars, that soft gloop of noise, that polite and plaintive singing. It's overwhelmed and anaethetised everything else. Smoothed off the edges. Made it all palatable and harmless and empty.

Likewise, Chris Martin himself doesn't seem even a quarter as bad as most of the other people in this book. People have made snide comments about his wealthy background – but that's hardly his fault. Cynics also raised eyebrows about his relationship with Gwyneth Paltrow – the clean-living, clean-eating Hollywood Star who'd have you believe that she farts perfumed rainbows. But really, that's Chris Martin's personal business. And even though plenty of people laughed when the two split up and talked about 'conscious uncoupling', at least they tried to handle their break-up with quiet dignity rather than hating each other all over the tabloids.

It's probably also only fair to admit that Chris Martin has campaigned hard for many years for fair trade, has rarely been publicly mean about anyone and has spoken up against racism in politics. He can even be funny and self-aware. He once told *Rolling Stone* magazine that he would give his 'left ball' to write anything as good as

Radiohead's *OK Computer*. He said of the Oxford band: 'Sometimes I feel like they cleared a path with a machete, and we came afterward and put up a strip mall.'

And it's hard to put it better than that. He took all the danger and made it into a shopper's paradise. He made it safe for corporations, comfortable for everyone – and completely boring. He paved the way for Ed Sheeran.

Music used to matter. It used to frighten people. It used to galvanise them into action. When the folksinger Woody Guthrie was blazing a trail to Bob Dylan, Bruce Springsteen and a better future with his songs of protest and frustration, he used to write on his guitar: 'This Machine Kills Fascists'. If Chris Martin has a message for us, it is 'Resistance Is Futile'.

SIMON COWELL

—

Date of birth: 7 October 1959
In a nutshell: Reality TV tsar
Connected to: David Cameron, Piers Morgan

When Simon Cowell appeared on *Desert Island Discs* he became the
first guest in the long history of the show to ask for a mirror as his
luxury item. Why did he want it? 'Because I'd miss me,' he said. He
said he wanted to look at himself – and it was hard to know how
seriously to take him.

The rest of his career has been a similarly perplexing blend of comedy
and sincerity. Did he mean it when he launched songs by the Power
Rangers on the UK charts? And two puppets called Zig and
Zag? And two actors called Robson and Jerome? Does he mean it on
his TV programmes when he says, 'I don't mean to be rude, but …'?
And does he mean it when he's subsequently as rude as he can
possibly be?

He's an enigma. And he's funny. And he's not funny. But whatever you do or don't make of him, there's no denying Simon Cowell's success. In the UK his artists released the two top-selling singles of the 2000s. By the time he left *American Idol*, the programme he co-devised and co-presented was on its seventh season in a row at the top of US primetime rankings. Other reality TV programmes of his, like *The X Factor* and *Britain's Got Talent*, have also been stunningly popular. He helped discover global phenomena like Susan Boyle and One Direction. And, okay, some people might argue that reality TV is corrosive in the way it pits people against each other. Others might say that Cowell has DESTROYED MUSIC along the way, encouraging histrionic warbling in place of true emotion, and encouraging his protégés to tear Leonard Cohen's beautiful song 'Hallelujah' to absolute shreds. But that's a matter of taste. And again, it's hard to know how seriously to take him – and how much to hold against him.

There have been times when Cowell has played it dead straight. Most notably his apparently sincere and public support of David Cameron came back to haunt him when Cameron scarpered from office immediately following the disaster of the EU referendum. Not least because Cowell had said: 'He has substance and the stomach to navigate us through difficult times.'

But the real worry about Simon Cowell is his influence. *Time* magazine put him in their top 100 most important people in 2004 and 2010. *The New Statesman* named him as one of the '50 people who matter' in 2010. A BBC Radio 4 series to mark the diamond jubilee of Elizabeth II named him as one of the people 'whose actions during the reign of Elizabeth II have had a significant impact on lives in these islands and given the age its character'.

This last accolade in particular provokes the question of how he might have given the age its character. Is the fact that we have a reality show TV star President of the USA somehow attributable to Simon

Cowell? What have his own TV programmes encouraged people to do? Has he taught very silly people around the world that they should vote according to prejudice, emotion and whatever drunken fancy takes them on a Saturday night? Just how seriously should we take him?

PIERS MORGAN

—

Date of birth: *30 March 1965*

In a nutshell: *Piers Moron*

Connected to: *Donald Trump, Simon Cowell*

Some things Piers Morgan has attacked:

J. K. Rowling
Emma Watson
Women in protest marches
Post-Traumatic Stress Disorder victims
Lady Gaga
Migrants
Journalists
Madonna

Morgan moaned on Twitter that J. K. Rowling is 'superior, dismissive and arrogant'. He claimed never to have read 'a single word' of Harry Potter – although Rowling was later able to produce an article Morgan himself had written praising the much-loved author's books for helping children 'to read, feel inspired and be creative'.

Emma Watson, he said, was guilty of being a hypocrite for taking part in a revealing photoshoot when she criticised Beyoncé for also appearing in provocative videos. Even though, it turned out, Watson had actually supported Beyoncé.*

Morgan described women who were protesting against Donald Trump as 'rabid feminists' and 'nasty'.

Post-Traumatic Stress Disorder, said Piers, is a 'celebrity accessory'.

Lady Gaga apparently deserved particular opprobrium for publicly saying she suffers from PTSD – even though she actually does, and was the victim of a rape.

Morgan has referred to a 'swarm' of 'migration through Europe'.

'All journalists', said the former newspaper editor, 'are hypocrites.' This is one of his better jokes.

On the subject of hypocrites, he said of Madonna: 'She has an opinion quota ... based on this pure ability to shock and offend, which I find pointless, quite clichéd and increasingly very nauseating.'

---

* She liked the fact she could both be an intellectual feminist and be okay with being pretty. It showed that there is a broad spectrum of female empowerment. This was too subtle for Piers.

Some things Piers Morgan has defended:

The right of employers to force women to wear high heels
*Julia Roberts for refusing to wear high heels on the red carpet
    at Cannes*
Brexit
Donald Trump
*Donald Trump's comments about wanting to punish women
    who have illegal abortions*
The Daily Mail
Waterboarding
Piers Morgan

Morgan doesn't find Brexit nauseating, even though he also says he didn't vote for it. Similarly, he says he wouldn't vote for Donald Trump, but he is his great friend. The *Daily Mail*, he says, is an addictive pleasure. He has also said: 'It's an arguable point as to whether waterboarding constitutes torture.'

There's no arguing when it comes to Piers Morgan, though. 'I was falsely accused,' he says, 'of ogling Susanna Reid's cleavage … I. Was. Eyeing. Her. Notes.'

Susanna Reid is Piers' long-suffering co-host on *Good Morning Britain*, the TV programme on which Morgan is most often seen bloviating here in the UK in 2017. Susanna Reid has said she sometimes cries at home because of Piers.

So how did this manifestly unqualified man get to have such a huge bully pulpit? Why is it that we get to hear so much about it when he defends the indefensible – or just as often attacks people who are either nicer or weaker than him?

It's a mystery that history cannot explain. Morgan's career has been one long and knotted string of inexplicable successes and catastrophic failures. After nearly a decade engaged in the tabloid equivalent of journalism, Piers disgraced himself in a scene that was to be replayed with subtle variations over the next twenty years when he was fired for publishing photographs of an aristocrat leaving an addictive disorders clinic – breaking the editors' code of conduct and trampling all over the privacy of a vulnerable young woman.

After that, Morgan became the editor of the *Daily Mirror*. Within a year, he was publicly apologising during the European football championship after running the headline 'ACHTUNG! SURRENDER! For you Fritz ze Euro 96 Championship is over'.* But in spite of such assaults on taste and international harmony, Morgan managed to remain in the editor's chair until 2004, when he was finally fired for authorising publication of fake photographs alleging to show Iraqi prisoners being abused by British soldiers.

Trinity Mirror Group later admitted that during Morgan's time at the *Mirror*, some of its journalists had been hacking phones. Morgan has always denied any involvement. But during the Leveson enquiry into the scandal, Morgan was heavily criticised by Lord Leveson himself, who said that Morgan's statements about hacking were 'utterly unpersuasive' and 'clearly prove … that he was aware that it was taking place in the press as a whole and that he was sufficiently unembarrassed by what was criminal behaviour that he was prepared to joke about it'.

In the years following his exit from the *Mirror* Morgan appeared on a number of TV programmes, proudly remembering in a *Mail on Sunday* article in 2009 that no less a personality than Jimmy Savile

---

* This headline ran the night before the game. Germany won on penalties. Not for the last time, Morgan's prediction had proved inaccurate.

came up to him and told him: "Your TV shows are BRILLIANT.' He also met Donald Trump when he appeared on the kingbaby's own show, *Celebrity Apprentice*. Since then, he's been one of Trump's staunchest allies and defenders in the press and on Twitter. 'I judge him for how he behaves as a campaigner and now as a president,' he once explained. And also, 'I like him.'

'If only you'd read Harry Potter,' said J. K. Rowling, 'you'd know the downside of sucking up to the biggest bully in school is getting burned alive.'

In spite of such sound advice, Morgan has remained undaunted. He's been so fulsome and repeated in his praise of Trump that when the president tweeted 'THE MOVEMENT CONTINUES' the footballer Gary Lineker felt compelled to respond that he hoped it wasn't a 'bowel movement' because 'Piers Morgan could fall out'.

That's right, Morgan has also made an enemy of football legend, Gary Lineker. Lineker is, you see, a 'goal-hanger'. Although as Lineker pointed out: 'Better to be a goal-hanger than a phone-hacker.'

But annoying intelligent and kindly national treasures like Gary Lineker and J. K. Rowling doesn't seem to bother Piers. 'I'm just putting opinions out there,' he said in an interview with the *Guardian*. 'It's my job.' And was he trying to get publicity for himself? 'Of course!' he said. 'Everyone on TV is. I'm just better at it than most of them.' That also is incorrect.

BORIS JOHNSON

Date of birth: *19 June 1964*

In a nutshell: *Eton mess*

Connected to: *David Cameron, Nigel Farage, Theresa May, Michael Gove*

Boris Johnson was attacked and derided when he gave his first press conference as British Foreign Secretary with his American counterpart John Kerry. Journalists asked why they should trust him, what they should make of the 'outright lies' he had told throughout his career, and if he recalled the many insults he'd levelled at other world leaders and their countries.

'There is a rich thesaurus of things that I have said that have, one way or the other, I don't know how, that has been misconstrued,' bumbled Boris. 'Most people, when they read these things in their proper context, can see what was intended.'

Let's provide some of that context now. In 1990, for instance, he was recorded talking to his old Eton and Oxford University friend (and later convicted fraudster) Darius Guppy. Guppy wanted Johnson to give him the contact details of another journalist so he could set heavies on him.

'My blood is up … There is nothing I won't do to get my revenge,' said Guppy.

'How badly are you going to hurt this guy?' asked Boris.

'Not badly at all.'

'I really want to know,' said Boris. (Are you letting in a chink of sympathy?)

'Look, let me explain to you …' said Guppy.

'If this guy sues me I will be fucking furious,' said Boris. (Oh well.)

Guppy eventually reassured Boris that the journalist would probably just get a couple of black eyes and a broken rib. Boris remained concerned that he might 'get in trouble', but eventually, said 'I'll do it.'

For the sake of context, it's worth noting that Guppy's plans didn't work out. The journalist wasn't beaten up. Perhaps Boris had been deceiving Guppy and didn't supply the particulars he wanted. Perhaps Guppy had second thoughts. But whatever it was that 'was intended', it wasn't good.

Mind you, in 1990, Boris had lots of other things on his mind. While that tape was being recorded Boris was working in Brussels for the *Daily Telegraph*, and busy developing two new journalistic genres that would change our lives forever: post-truth and the Euromyth.

'Threat to British pink sausages'; 'Brussels recruits sniffers to ensure that Euro-manure smells the same' ran the headlines on Boris's popular dispatches from the Belgian capital. 'Snails are fish, says EU.'

Of course, that wasn't quite what the EU said. And Boris got quite a reputation for telling stretchers. So outrageous were his porkies that James Landale, a fellow Brussels correspondent, was moved to verse, in a parody of Hilaire Belloc's *Matilda*. 'Boris told such dreadful lies,' he wrote, 'It made one gasp and stretch one's eyes.'

But Boris knew he was onto something. These stories of out-of-control bureaucracy were just what Torygraph readers wanted to hear. It might have been complete Horlicks, but it fed their prejudices. More than that, it helped create an image of the EU that has been prevalent in the UK ever since. Not least because Boris has kept hard at it. When he betrayed his Prime Minister David Cameron and declared his hand in the referendum for Leave, he proudly reminisced in the *Telegraph* about 'ludicrous' EU rules: 'like the rule that you can't recycle a teabag, or that children under eight cannot blow up balloons'.

It's true at least that the rules sound daft. Typically, the rest is nonsense. There are no rules about children blowing up balloons or any of us recycling teabags. But Boris has never been one to let the facts get in the way of a good story. He explained to the BBC that during his time in Brussels:

'[I] was sort of chucking these rocks over the garden wall. And I listened to this amazing crash from the greenhouse next door over in England as everything I wrote from Brussels was having this amazing, explosive effect on the Tory party – and it really gave me this, I suppose, rather weird sense of power.'

Boris enjoyed the weird power so much that his next move was into politics. He became an MP for the safe Tory seat of Henley in 2001.

By May 2004 he had risen to be the Shadow Minister for Arts. By November he had been sacked. Johnson had dismissed allegations that he had been having an affair as an 'inverted pyramid of piffle' – but as usual it was he himself who had been over-liberal with the truth and his leader told him to step down.

Yet somehow, Boris carried on. In 2008 he became Mayor of London, where he set about disfiguring London's skyline with dozens of phallic skyscrapers. He also built absurd white elephants like a £60 million cable car across the river. In 2013, just four commuters used this bizarre device often enough to qualify for a regular users' discount. Four. In a city of 8.6 million.

Boris's relationship with the truth also grew still more estranged during his tenure in London. As well as spreading the usual manure, he started concealing facts. Most notoriously, he failed to publish a report that said 433 primary schools in London were being exposed to dangerous levels of air pollution. Which is worth saying again. Children were being poisoned, with lifelong consequences. And rather than doing something about it, Boris kept the evidence from his electorate.

And then there came the Brexit campaign, in which Boris repeatedly appeared in front of a bus claiming 'we send the EU £350 million a week'. Which was untrue. And also in front of signs saying, 'Let's give our NHS the £350 million the EU takes every week.' Which no one had any intention of doing.

And yet still, in spite of everything, he became the UK foreign secretary and got to appear alongside John Kerry and other world leaders. Blond and scruffy and smiling, a giant and terrifying metaphor for our age, a man who lies as easily and happily as a dog licks his balls, representing his country at one of the most delicate points in its history. Jean-Marc Ayrault – the French foreign minister – complained that the EU would need a negotiating partner who had not 'lied a lot' and who was 'clear, credible and reliable'. But how naïve was Ayrault? That sounds far too sensible. It's never going to happen. It's Boris's world now. We're just living in it.

Learn about nations and their leaders with Foreign Secretary Boris Johnson!

- President Putin is 'a ruthless and manipulative tyrant'.
- Donald Trump is 'out of his mind' and exhibits 'stupefying ignorance'.
- Barack Obama is 'downright hypocritical'.
- 'Chinese cultural influence,' he says 'is virtually nil, and unlikely to increase.'
- On the Commonwealth he says: 'It is said that the Queen has come to love the Commonwealth, partly because it supplies her with regular cheering crowds of flag-waving piccaninnies.'
- When Tony Blair went to visit the Congo, he said: 'The tribal warriors will all break out in watermelon smiles to see the big white chief touch down in his big white British taxpayer-funded bird.'

MICHAEL GOVE

—

Date of birth: *26 August 1967*
In a nutshell: *Not an expert*
Connected to: *Boris Johnson, Theresa May, David Cameron*

'People in this country have had enough of experts,' said Michael Gove during the Brexit referendum campaign. It was an astonishing and depressing … let's say, moment. I was about to write 'admission', but there was no admitting about it. Gove seemed proud to say that experts should be derided, that people had been turned against them. There was even a hint of venom in his voice. He was annoyed. His interviewer, Faisal Islam, had forced Gove to admit that he couldn't name an economist who supported his assertion that Britain would be 'freer, fairer and better off' for leaving the EU. There had also been painful discussion because many experts had (correctly, as it turned out) suggested that the NHS would never get the £350 million extra money a week that Gove's campaign was promising after the UK left the EU.

But Gove's irritation with experts was more than just a momentary flash of anger. He had other good reasons to be fed up with all those clever people who actually know things. For almost his entire career these pesky experts been telling Gove he was wrong. More than wrong. That he was entirely unsuited to doing his job. When he was Secretary of Education, the Association of Head Teachers, the Association of Teachers and Lecturers, the National Union of Teachers, the National Association of Schoolmasters and the National Union of Women Teachers all voted that they had no confidence in Gove. In other words, a large percentage of the clever people in the country pointed their brains at him and found him lacking. Worse still, experts also often suggested that he was inhumane. The Association of Head Teachers said that he had fostered a 'climate of bullying, fear and intimidation'. Meanwhile, in a separate judicial review in 2011, a judge declared that his failure to consult before imposing cuts on school building projects was 'so unfair as to amount to an abuse of power'.

But Gove gave as good as he got when he was Education Secretary. He might not have had any expert knowledge or research on his side, but he did have a rock-solid faith in his own opinion. And one of the things he learned after carefully consulting the inside of his own head was that schools were overcome by 'anti-knowledge' culture and that this was a very bad thing.

Those seeing an apparent contradiction here would be right – but some of the rough edges are smoothed off once you realise that what Gove meant by 'knowledge' generally turned out to be a load of old nonsense. 'What [students] need is a rooting in the basic scientific principles, Newton's laws of thermodynamics,' Gove once explained, unaware that the laws of thermodynamics were slated in various forms by a number of people during the nineteenth century, before being formulated as the four laws known today. But no matter. Gove plunged on. He also developed a new history curriculum. He originally stated that he was going to employ the 'expert' help of popular historian Simon Schama in this great work. But Schama was unavailable. Although he did pass comment on the end results: he characterised Gove's proposals as 'insulting and offensive' and 'pedantic and utopian', and said Gove had constructed a 'ridiculous shopping list' of subjects.

Those pesky experts! No matter. Gove still continued. One of his biggest gifts to the nation was to destroy the childhood of everyone at school by forcing them to sit extra exams and learn bizarre new grammar rules about 'fronted adverbials', 'noun-phrases', 'determiners', 'present progressives', 'past progressives' and 'dangling participles'. And if you're wondering what all that stuff means, just imagine how much six-year-olds enjoy learning this arcane code. Imagine how they feel trying to apply such terms to English, a language that has always stoutly resisted grammatical certainty and fixed rules … As any expert could have told Gove, if only he had listened.

And so, on he pobbed to the EU referendum. In that same Faisal Islam interview he declared that he had no interest in becoming the leader of the Tory party. 'Count me out,' he said. True to form, a few weeks later he was counting himself in, withdrawing his support from his friend Boris Johnson the morning he was due to declare his own hand. Boris's leadership bid collapsed. You could possibly reckon that as the one good thing Gove has done for us – if only he hadn't thereby delivered us Theresa May.

THERESA MAY

—

Date of birth: 1 October 1956
In a nutshell: Took control of the Brexit bus and drove it off a cliff, with us in it
Connected to: Nigel Farage, Marine Le Pen, Donald Trump, Jeremy Corbyn,
David Cameron

There's little doubt that Theresa May was handed a shit sandwich when she took over as UK Prime Minister. There was chaos and uncertainty following the narrow win for the leave vote in the UK Brexit referendum and in the wake of David Cameron's sudden resignation. There would be years' worth of hard yakka ahead. And no one knew what leaving the European Union would actually mean. Least of all her.

But it's hard to feel too sympathetic. Not least because May has spent so much of her time in power insisting that we all eat the sandwich too. And not only that – saying that if we don't tuck in with sufficient relish we are 'talking down' the country. We all need to get behind this shit-sandwich eating, she says. And those who would rather not eat wet faeces wrapped up in bread that suddenly costs twice as much as it did last year are 'denying the will of the people'.

As well as forcing us to feast on turds, Theresa May has produced a fair bit of her own dung. Since assuming power, May has insisted that it is the will of her British volk to reduce immigration and has set us on a course to leave the free market for the sake of controlling our borders. She neglects to mention that she was previously in charge of these borders in her role as home secretary – and that the main reason her government persistently failed to meet its pledges to reduce the number of people arriving in Britain was because of the arrivals of non-Europeans. Three-quarters of all immigrants to the UK since 1990 have arrived from outside the EU. What's more, the main reason so many immigrants came here is that we have a labour market that is more lightly regulated than those of our European friends. Thanks, in other words, to Conservative Party policies.

Yet while May failed to do anything to limit the number of new arrivals, she did do plenty to stir up hatred and resentment against our new neighbours. She sent vans around London in 2013 carrying billboards telling illegal immigrants to 'go home or face arrest'. A move so sinister that even Nigel Farage said she'd gone a bit far. She announced a policy asking landlords to carry out checks on the immigration status of their tenants. The former Deputy Prime Minister of the UK, Nick Clegg, has also accused her of manipulating government reports to remove information about the benefits of immigration.

Tellingly, at the Conservative Party Conference in 2011, May cited the case of a foreign national who was allowed to remain in the UK under the terms of the European Human Rights Act 'because – and I am not making this up – he had a pet cat'.

But she *was* making it up. The actual reason the man had been allowed to stay was that he was in a relationship with a British person

– and the pet cat was just a piece of evidence that had been cited to prove that their love was genuine. May's comments 'had been laughable and childlike', said veteran Tory MP Kenneth Clarke.

After the referendum, when May was in the running for the leadership of the Tory party, Clarke was also caught on camera explaining to a friend that she was a 'bloody difficult woman'. The aides of her erstwhile party leader David Cameron, meanwhile, called her 'submarine May' during the referendum campaign because it was so hard to find her. She never seemed to be around when they needed support … A cynic would have thought she was hedging her bets, just in case Cameron came a cropper and she got her chance to make a leadership bid. But that's not to say that she didn't have strong opinions. She was recorded making a speech to Goldman Sachs bankers in which she stated there were 'clear' economic arguments for remaining in the EU and that 'there are definite benefits for us'.

Oh well. Maybe she changed her mind after the result came in – but if she did, it just adds to the hypocrisy of her subsequent steely-eyed insistence that there is no turning back and no one else can have second thoughts about Brexit.

Not that her hard line bothers her new fans on the international stage. 'She's running the UK using policies that I want to run,' said the French fascist leader Marine Le Pen. Donald Trump also famously invited her over to Washington within days of his inauguration. They held hands. He declared, 'Brexit is going to be wonderful.' She hitched the UK's wagon onto this foaming bucking bronco. She invited him over to the UK for a state visit. And the next day Trump enacted his 'Muslim ban' and new restrictions on travel into the USA that saw families suddenly divided, and long-term US residents facing alienation from their homes and uncertain futures. A policy that unleashed riots, protest and division. Small wonder he and May got on so well.

When Nicola Sturgeon demanded a referendum on Scottish independence in March 2017, days after May had forced the bill that enacted the outcome of the EU referendum vote through Parliament, Theresa May said: 'I think it wouldn't be fair to the people of Scotland because they're being asked to make a crucial decision without all the necessary information – without knowing what the future partnership would be, or what the alternative of an independent Scotland would look like.' Yes she did. She said that.

MARINE LE PEN

Date of birth: 5 August 1968
In a nutshell: *Can smile and smile and be a villain*
Connected to: *Vladimir Putin, Nigel Farage, Theresa May*

When Donald Trump won the US election, the vice president of the French fascist party, the Front National, tweeted a photo of Marine Le Pen with the caption, 'Their world is collapsing. Ours is being built.'

Marine Le Pen's father, Jean-Marie Le Pen added: 'Today the United States, tomorrow France.'

A few months earlier, Marine Le Pen had glowingly compared Brexit to the trotting-runs, saying: 'The UK has begun a movement that can't be stopped.'

And back on US election night, Nicolas Bay, her party's secretary general, was also convinced that Trump and Brexit helped Le Pen's cause. 'It shows French people that there's a patriotic dynamic that goes well beyond France. There's a springtime of the people.'

Anyone who has had the pleasure of watching Mel Brooks' classic film *The Producers* will also remember the song 'Springtime for Hitler'. But evocations of World War II are probably coincidental. The subject has been a tricky one for Le Pen and her party over the years. She likes to claim her anti-immigration party, which has claimed Islam is incompatible with French values, is 'not racist' and that this charge has been levelled at her by the 'elites'. But she also once faced charges of inciting racism for commenting:

'For those who want to talk a lot about World War II, if it's about occupation, then we could also talk about it [Muslim prayers in the streets], because that is occupation of territory ...'

Of course, she could have argued that she wasn't saying anything so bad. Her father, after all, had previously claimed that the Nazi occupation of France was not 'particularly inhumane'.* Mind you, Le Pen senior had also described the gas chambers as 'a detail of the history of World War II'. His loose tongue and rabid anti-Semitism even eventually got too much for the image-conscious Marine, who dismissed him from the Front National in 2015. But not before she had managed several of Jean-Marie's presidential campaigns. And not without keeping the essential structures and aims of the party he once ran.

In fact, the Front National is so toxic that even Nigel Farage used to keep his distance, saying her party was too full of 'prejudice' and 'anti-Semitism' even for him. But he changed his tune soon after he

---

* Just in case you need reminding: almost 80,000 French Jews were killed in the war. 80,000 men, women and children. Thousands of other civilians were also murdered. On 10 June 1944, for instance, SS soldiers killed every man, woman and child they could find in the village of Oradour-sur-Glane. They killed over 400 people who were sheltering in a church by burning it down, and machine-gunned those who tried to escape the flames.

left frontline politics to take up a new position inside Donald Trump's rectum. More recently he has been seen interviewing Marine Le Pen on LBC.

Curiously, although he invited her to sing Putin's praises* in this interview, Farage didn't manage to ask Marine Le Pen about the Front National's ongoing legal troubles. He didn't take the opportunity to ask how it was that her party, which has stood on an anti-corruption ticket, ended up with officials facing trial for overcharging the state for campaign expenses during the 2012 election. Nor did he enquire about all the other allegations of illegal funding relating to the Front National. Or about the fact that French prosecutors were currently investigating Le Pen for distributing violent images taken by Islamic State militants and showing the murder of French citizens.

But in spite of Farage's best efforts, there was one interesting moment in the interview. Le Pen briefly let her mask slip when she started to blame the 'Anglo-Saxon world' for the 'design of free trade and globalisation and blurred borders'. Farage turned red, and laughed awkwardly and tried to interrupt, but she continued to talk about the evils of 'Anglo-Saxon' liberalisation. Eventually he managed to get a word in and say, 'I don't think the Anglo-Saxons should take all the blame …'

In those few moments it had become clear that for all their talk of common ground, Farage and Le Pen's nationalisms – as all nationalisms must – left them fundamentally opposed. She was only for the French, and so against the 'Anglo-Saxons'. He is only for the English. For now, that means he hates on Brussels. But you could see in Le Pen's wolf smile that she knew where all this was heading. If the Front

---

* Le Pen has been loaned millions of euros by Russian banks. She says that these loans do not compromise her leadership. She has also frequently publicly defended the Russian dictator and said she admires him.

National get to build their world, there will be no common ground between nations. All such friendships will collapse. We'll just have to hope the fallout isn't 'particularly inhumane'.

PAUL DACRE

Date of birth: *14 November 1948*

In a nutshell: Daily Mail *editor*

Connected to: *Adolf Hitler, Katie Hopkins*

Paul Dacre is the editor of the *Daily Mail* and has been since 1992.

In 1997, the *Daily Mail* ran an article saying the Labour MP Mo Mowlam looked like an 'only slightly effeminate Geordie trucker' because she appeared to be wearing a wig and had recently gained a lot of weight. Mo Mowlam had put on weight and lost her hair thanks to the treatment she was undergoing for cancer.

In 2011, the *Daily Mail* misquoted a survey in order to suggest that 'the changing role of women in our society' causes autism.

In 2011, the *Daily Mail*'s website (briefly) ran a story about Amanda Knox's appeal in the Meredith Kercher case. The story said that Knox had been found guilty of the murder and described her 'stunned' face. Gleeful comments were provided from 'prosecutors' who said they were 'delighted' by the result. The only trouble was that the *Mail* had published too early. Knox was innocent. The quotes were fabricated.

In 2012, the *Daily Mail* ran a story claiming oral sex is good for women's health and fights depression. They had, again, misquoted a survey.

In January 2014, the *New Statesman* journalist Peter Wilby noted that just before the Press Complaints Commission closed down, the *Daily Mail* had received 687 complaints that led to a PCC adjudication or negotiated resolution, far more than any other paper. In 2013 alone, said Wilby, the *Mail* falsely reported that 878,000 benefit recipients had stopped claiming their allowance once they were told they had to 'face a fresh medical'; that pupils in Portsmouth had been denied water on the hottest day of the year because of Ramadan; that almost half of the electricity generated by windfarms wasn't used; that asylum seekers had 'targeted' Scotland; that disabled babies were being euthanised by a palliative care service. They also falsely reported that wolves were about to be returned to the UK. (Who knows why?)

In the same year, the *Mail* also said that the EU was proposing to ban books like Enid Blyton's Famous Five series because they portrayed 'traditional' families. (I think we can guess why.)

In 2015, the *Daily Mail* ran a story claiming Israel was intentionally opening dams in the south of the country in order to flood the Gaza Strip. Even though there are no dams in southern Israel. (Don't start guessing. The implications are too horrible.)

In 2016, in the run-up to the EU referendum in 2016, the *Daily Mail* claimed that 'Brussels Bureaucrats' 'could' be about to impose taxes on dustbins and on driving through 'ALL towns and cities'. There were no plans to enforce these ideas. The *Daily Mail* ran a front-page splash about migrants found hiding in the back of a lorry headlined by the quotation 'We're From Europe – Let Us In'. The men were from Iraq and Kuwait. The *Daily Mail* ran an editorial claiming 'we do less than 10 per cent' of our total business with the EU, when the EU accounts for 44 per cent of our exports alone. The *Daily Mail* also claimed that free movement was depressing wages. It wasn't. It claimed that the EU was going to build an army – which it couldn't do without the UK's consent. (So long as the UK remained a member, anyway.) It claimed the EU is run by a 'secretive, unelected commission', even though the power to pass legislation in the EU rests with an elected parliament. At the top of an article about a speech by the US Director of National Intelligence, the *Daily Mail* ran a headline claiming that ISIS had 'taken advantage' of Europe's open borders to plant 'sleeper cells' in the UK. This was not true. The *Daily Mail* also ran an article based on a speech by UK justice minister Dominic Raab, saying 'Britain could stop ten times more terror suspects' from entering the UK if it left the EU. This was not true. The *Daily Mail* ran an article claiming that a 'massive influx of EU migrants' had forced doctors to take on 1.5 million extra patients in three years and that the NHS was at 'breaking point'. This was not true. The *Daily Mail* ran an article saying 700 EU migrants were convicted of crimes in the UK 'every week'. This was not true.

In 2017, and perhaps not surprisingly, Wikipedia banned the *Daily Mail* as an 'unreliable source'. Its contributors were told not to use *Daily Mail* articles for reference (other than in exceptional circumstances) because of their reputation 'for poor fact checking, sensationalism and flat-out fabrication'.

Paul Dacre is the editor of the *Daily Mail*. Few people have more influence over UK culture and discourse. Politicians fear him. His editorial line directs national policy. Paul Dacre is the editor of the *Daily Mail*.

In 1934, the *Daily Mail* ran an article written by its owner Viscount Rothermere headlined 'Hoorah for the Blackshirts!' and declaring support for Oswald Mosley's British fascist party. In 1939, he also wrote to Hitler commending him for his 'superhuman' efforts in 'regenerating' his country. Viscount Rothermere's direct descendant still owns the *Daily Mail*. He has non-domicile UK tax status. The *Daily Mail* has run hundreds of articles about 'benefits scroungers', 'health tourism' and foreigners abusing British tax-payers' money.

KATIE HOPKINS

Date of birth: *13 February 1975*

In a nutshell: *The world's worst columnist*

Connected to: *Paul Dacre, Donald Trump*

According to Donald Trump, the *Daily Mail* writer Katie Hopkins is a 'respected columnist'. According to Katie Hopkins herself, meanwhile, she is nothing less than a 'conduit for truth.'

And if truth were a river of poo, she'd be right. As it is, the sewerage and inaccuracies that flow from her mouth have an awkward habit of being proven, well, untrue.

In March 2017, the cook and blogger Jack Monroe won £24,000 damages (with more than £100,000 in legal expenses also added to the bill) after being incorrectly accused by Hopkins of vandalising a war memorial. A few months earlier, in December 2016, the *Daily Mail* also had to pay out £150,000 after Hopkins falsely accused a British Muslim family of extremism. She said that two brothers who were stopped on the way to Disneyland with their children had links to Al Qaeda and that US authorities were right to stop them. She said they weren't on their way to Disneyland – that this was a lie – and that one of the brothers had also set up a Facebook page full of extremist material. In all of these things her conduit was cloacal.

As well as the damages, Hopkins and the *Mail* were asked to make an apology to the aggrieved family. Katie made hers on Twitter at 2 am. Perhaps she did it when everyone was sleeping because she was embarrassed? No, not by the inaccurate accusation. But because back in 2015, at a church conference in London she'd roundly declared: 'I have never apologised for anything I've said. I find it very disappointing when people apologise. You should have the positive moral attitude to stand by what you say.'

At the same meeting, she'd appealed to the religious in the crowd by explaining, 'I am the Jesus of the outspoken. Jesus had his followers – I have 600,000 followers on Twitter. It's about leading the way – I am the new Jesus.'

This remarkable speech was something of a high-water mark for the outspoken Brexit campaigner's effluence. Other doozies included:

'I don't see how I've incited hatred. I point out solutions – send gunboats to the Med, blow up the boats, keep people on shore, look after people in situ.'

And:

'I don't believe in food banks at all … I don't believe we are all equal. It's fundamentally stupid if you can't afford to feed your family but you have an iPhone 6. All the kids on free school meals have iPhones.'

She also explained that she was intending to write a new Christmas book called *The Bible*, apparently innocent of the fact that there was another Christmas-themed book with the same title. Alas, little has been heard of her religious masterpiece since. But we've heard plenty from Katie Hopkins. She has become a mirror of our times: someone who first rose to fame from being rude to people on a reality TV programme called *The Apprentice*, and has since parlayed that infamy into ever more influence and cash. She's called for the peers in the British House of Lords to be gassed. She's said she'd like to see euthanasia-vans – a bit like 'ice-cream vans' going around dealing with the fact that 'we just have far too many old people'. She's said that 'being depressed' is 'a fashionable thing to be'. She's also told viewers of ITV's *This Morning* that she doesn't like her children to play with children with 'lower-class' names like Charmaine, Chantelle or Tyler.

All of which sounds like so much liberal-baiting nonsense. It's easy to dismiss her as a professional troll who hates for cash. It's fun too. Swatting the 'queen of mean' has become a kind of national sport on Twitter in the UK. But the trouble is that Hopkins can't be so easily ignored and dismissed. The fact that she spreads her dung on national television and in widely read newspapers isn't just a symptom of the moral decay eating at the heart of the country – it's a contributory factor. Every time Katie Hopkins says something awful, she moves the boundaries on what people are used to seeing and prepared to accept. She's also shown that you can get paid to move those perceptions. She's made cruelty into a profitable sport. And she's hurt a lot of people in the process. Never more so than when she wrote that she didn't care about migrants dying on the sea. 'Make no mistake,' she said, 'these migrants are like cockroaches. They might look a bit "Bob Geldof's Ethiopia circa 1984", but they are built to survive a nuclear bomb.'

Cockroach was a term used both by the Nazis and in the Rwandan genocide. The UN High Commissioner for Human Rights Zeid Ra'ad al-Hussein responded: 'This type of language is clearly inflammatory and unacceptable, especially in a national newspaper.'

It was only a few months later that Trump was praising Hopkins as a respected columnist, and thanking her for her 'powerful writing' on the UK's 'Muslim problem'. Hopkins was so delighted that she said she'd move over to the USA if Trump won the election.

This too, alas, turned out to be untrue.

THE QUEEN

Date of birth: *21 April 1926*
In a nutshell: *Accident of birth*
Connected to: *David Cameron, Theresa May*

If there's virtue in living for a long time and saying little, then the Queen of England is some kind of saint. Give or take the occasional refusal to pay income tax, or the odd failure to register much sympathy when her daughter-in-law died, the Queen has given the British press remarkably little to gab about during her seventy-plus years' reign.

But doing nothing can also be a failing – especially when that lack of action helps reinforce an unfair status quo. She might not like Nicholas Witchell,* but nor has she done anything to stop the BBC's royal correspondent from fawning and scraping. Nor any of the other sycophants that surround her. She has inflicted hours of boredom on

---

* Or at least, her son Prince Charles doesn't. Referring to the BBC royal correspondent, he once said: 'These bloody people. I can't bear that man. I mean, he's so awful, he really is.'

the nation and strange men droning in awe for countless hours. By doing so she has also tacitly encouraged lickspittle deference.

More urgently, for the entire second half of the twentieth century, and now also a good part of the twenty-first, the Queen has been there to remind us that we do not live in a meritocracy. Her presence alone informs her subjects that no matter how hard they work, how clever they are or how good they are to other people, there will always be someone above them. Someone who didn't work to get there. Someone who was just born there. She has reinforced and symbolised a system that gives precedence to poshos. She has legitimised a world where those born without a silver spoon are counted and treated as lesser citizens. She has done nothing to address the idea that there might be something wrong with our top-heavy, iniquitous society, where accidents of birth make far more difference to the way you end up than anything you actually do.

Talking of iniquity, meanwhile, just because the Queen has been good at avoiding personal controversy, that doesn't mean she hasn't been busy. The Queen has had other interests alongside touring the nations of the world while looking grumpy. She has been very good both at making money – and making sure that none of her people get their hands on it.

In 1993 the Queen's finances came under the spotlight following an unfortunate fire at Windsor Castle. When it became clear that the public didn't much fancy footing the entire bill for repairs to her private house, there was a prolonged discussion of her wealth and finances, during which the unfortunate issue of taxation came up. It turned out that the Queen hadn't ever paid any. So she agree to a private arrangement whereby she would voluntarily pay undisclosed sums to the tax office (or, to give its full title, Her Majesty's Revenue and Customs). Which is worth repeating. She still hasn't been compelled to pay tax. And we don't know how much she's paying.

Aside from that one chink of light stemming from 1993, we've never managed to claw back any of her huge inherited and state-earned wealth. We don't even know how much she's got. Although we do know that she's getting more of it, all the time.

The Queen's people claim that a big part of her wealth – the Crown Estate – the lands and businesses that generate her income, don't actually belong to her. 'You would be hiding behind nomenclature and history to suggest that the Crown Estate is in any way an asset of the Queen's,' a palace spokesman claimed recently. Prompting the question of who it belongs to in that case. Does it belong to the public? And can we have some of the money in that case? No? Thought not.

In 2013, under the Coalition government, while austerity was wreaking havoc all over the country and most public servants were enduring years of pay freezes, the Queen managed to get a deal whereby each year she would be paid 15 per cent of the income from the (supposedly) publicly owned land and property in the Crown Estate – unless that income fell, in which case she'd still be given more than the year before.* Which is to say, she was guaranteed pay rises in perpetuity. Given the way the income of the Crown Estate has been rocketing year on year since the early 1980s, she was guaranteed healthy ones. In 2015 she netted a tasty £40 million. (Oh, and she also cost the taxpayer round about another £100 million in security and unknown millions more in travel expenses.)

On top of this income provided by her grateful public, there's also the money the Queen has tied up in private lands, her art collections and her many other assets. Reuters estimated in 2015 that she's worth

---

* In early 2017, a tiny committee of MPs also took a full thirteen minutes to decide to raise the per cent income from the Crown Estate from 15 to 25 until 2027, to pay for repairs to Buckingham Palace.

round about £22.8 billion pounds. To put that another way, that's enough to send the NHS £350 million a week for a year. Or it's over £300 for each of her subjects in the UK. But, of course, we can't have any of it. We don't deserve it. We weren't born right. We aren't royal.

YOUR GRANNY

Date of birth: *1946–1964*

In a nutshell: *The worst generation*

Connected to: *You*

I know. I loved my grannies too and they loved me. Plenty of old ladies are just wonderful. But still, survey after survey shows that if she's aged between sixty and eighty, your granny probably lives in a very nice house, that she certainly had all the benefits of the welfare state and European citizenship while young, but that she has also systematically taken them away from you by ensuring endless Tory election victories and, quite possibly, voting for Brexit.

What's more, she still thinks that you just need to work harder, show some discipline and stop moaning. So, fuck your granny.

As young adults, baby boomers started out with free education, paid apprenticeships, and work contracts that lasted on average more than ten years. Millennials start with an average of £20,000 student debt and their average job lasts fifteen months.

According to YouGov, 71 per cent of 18–24-year-olds voted to remain in the EU during the Brexit referendum. Sixty-four per cent of those aged over 65 voted to leave. And 60 per cent of those aged 50–64.

In the USA, exit poll data showed that 55 per cent of 18–24-year-olds voted for Hillary Clinton (versus 37 per cent for Trump). Fifty-three per cent of those aged 65 and above voted for Trump (versus 45 per cent for Clinton).

In 2016 the UK average house price was £205,000. In 1975, it was £10,388 (£89,242 in 2016 money). For first-time buyers the average house price is now more than five times average earnings. Back in 1983, it was less than three times the average income.

Baby boomers in America currently account for 40 per cent of the population – and 70 per cent of the wealth. In the UK, they own four-fifths of national assets.

JOHN ROMULUS BRINKLEY

—

Date of birth/death: *8 July 1885 – 26 May 1942*
In a nutshell: *Quack doctor turned wacky politician*
Connected to: *Adolf Hitler*

John Romulus Brinkley was a doctor. Except, he wasn't. He had some medical training, but he bought his medical degree from a diploma mill glorying in the name of the Kansas City Eclectic University, in 1915.

But that's not why he's so fascinating.

He's interesting because of what he did a few years later, after he had established a clinic in a small rural Kansas town called Milford. Brinkley's big moment came when a patient came to him complaining he was 'a flat tire'. Which is to say, impotent. Brinkley would later write that he reluctantly told the man there was nothing he could do for him, but that then the two fell to chatting. For some reason the subject of goats came up, and the fact that billy goats were always ready for action. Brinkley cracked a joke about putting 'a pair of those buck glands in you'. Immediately, the patient began to beg him to perform the operation. So Brinkley did. Yes, he did. He put goat testes in the man's own ball-sack.

Stranger still, people began to think this was a good idea. Miraculously, the patient's wife gave birth to a baby boy and soon Brinkley was declaring his goat-gonads treatment a universal panacea, saying it cured all manner of ailments in both men and women. So many people started demanding the operation that Brinkley ran out of goats – and patients had to bring their own. He even carried out his operation on one of the editors of the *Los Angeles Times*. The editor survived (in the short term), the operation was considered a success, and there came more publicity and more and more patients. Brinkley became very rich. He charged top dollar to perform his nutty operations and Milford was flooded with people sold on the idea that their problems might be so easily solved.

The fake doctor thought about opening a clinic in LA, but the State of California wisely refused to recognise his medical certification, declaring his resume to be riddled with 'lies and discrepancies' – so Brinkley determined that people should continue to come and see him in Kansas instead. And he had a great new way of reeling them in.

While he'd been in LA, Brinkley had seen an early radio station and realised that the new technology had huge untapped potential as an advertising medium. In 1923 he set up his own commercial station – the world's first – KFKB ('Kansas First, Kansas Best'). He used the airwaves to shamelessly market his goat-gland treatments, preying on the sexual and physical insecurities of his listeners. But along the way he also invented a whole new format, mixing his adverts with weather reports for his rural audience, with fundamentalist preaching, with long homely chats in his sonorous voice and with early country music (another first). Brinkley became famous.

Agents from California who were clamping down on diploma mills came to arrest him in 1924, but by that time he was so rich, bringing in so much money from medical tourism and donating so much money to his local town, that the governor of Kansas refused to let them take him. 'We people here in Kansas get fat on his medicine,' he said. 'We're going to keep him here so long as he lives.'

Okay. You might now be thinking Brinkley provides some kind of all-encompassing metaphor for everything else in this book. It's hard not to draw parallels from this man who invented commercial talk radio and commercial religious radio, who inadvertently popularised country music, who was obsessed by impotence and who bilked thousands of people out of their money by giving them goat balls. But hold off! There's more …

Brinkley carried on, pumping out the radio adverts and pumping up the balls of thousands of citizens. He sometimes performed the operation when drunk. He often performed it in less-than-sterile conditions. He knew it was entirely bogus, but who was going to say so? His patients either enjoyed a placebo effect, or were too embarrassed by the sexual nature of their treatments to go public. Few of us would like to admit to having allowed someone to put goat balls into our body, after all.

But things came to a head after Brinkley started inviting people to write in to his radio show with their medical problems – and prescribed treatments for them on air. Treatments, not coincidentally, that involved buying his own patent medicines (often little more than coloured water, but sometimes dangerously poisonous) from approved pharmacies. He started making yet more money – but now the body count was rising. It's known that forty-two people died in his clinics alone – but hundreds, possibly thousands more must have expired after he let them walk out with goat balls, or prescribed them dodgy medicines on air. In 1930, the Kansas Medical Board revoked his (fake!) licence to practise medicine and the Federal Radio Commission also moved against his radio station.

But before the authorities managed to shut him down, Brinkley made an audacious move. He stood for election as governor of Kansas. The story is a familiar one. The political establishment didn't take him seriously at first. He would rant and rave at his rallies. He declared he had suffered 'persecution no more justified than the persecution of Christ'. He promoted contradictory policies. He promised to combat the drought in Kansas by putting a new lake in every county, although he never explained how he would do it or how the lakes would work. But Brinkley had huge advantages. He had a new way of talking directly to rural voters with his radio show, he whizzed around in his private plane, he dazzled people with his wealth and his attacks on the establishment …

I know! You're thinking he's a metaphor again. But wait. Brinkley didn't actually win the election. He filed his application too late for his name to be printed on voting slips and so became a write-in candidate. Three days before the election, the Kansas Attorney General announced that rules for such candidates had changed and that in order for their vote to count, people had to spell their chosen candidate's name correctly. Bad news for a radio star with a poorly educated constituency. More than 50,000 ballots were discounted by the new rules – and Brinkley narrowly lost.

But he wasn't done yet. He moved to Texas and set up a radio station just over the border in Mexico to get around his broadcasting ban. He installed a transmitter so powerful that it made locals' bedsprings hum and their car lights flash on and off. He started beaming out his adverts all over the USA – and started allowing other quacks and hucksters to advertise on his airwaves. He became more famous and richer than ever. He had his name emblazoned on the side of his Cadillac and displayed in lights on the side of his giant pink mansion.

He also took a trip to Europe where he found Hitler's ideas chimed perfectly with his own increasingly rabid anti-Semitism. When he returned he had his swimming pool lined with swastikas.

Now, at last Brinkley really was a metaphor for our times.

But he does at least offer us some hope. Because his vanity eventually caused his own downfall. Throughout his long, nefarious career, the fake doctor had been dogged by Morris Fishbein of the American Medical Association. It was he who had provided the evidence to Californian legislators when Brinkley failed to get a licence there, and he who had helped move the actions that forced his nemesis out of Kansas.

In 1938, Fishbein had the genius idea of outrageously libelling the quack, writing a series of articles denouncing Brinkley as a 'charlatan', impugning his character and detailing the crimes in his career. Brinkley took the bait and sued. The case was a sensation. Things quickly turned against the goat-gonad pioneer when it became clear that he didn't even know the quantities of ingredients that went into most of his medicines and it was shown that there were no proofs for the efficacy of his procedures. The jury stated he 'should be considered a charlatan and a quack in the ordinary, well-understood meaning of those words'.

The word was out – finally and undeniably. Immediately, hundreds of former patients sued him for malpractice, the IRS began to investigate him for tax evasion and the Post Office Department for mail fraud.

He was declared bankrupt and died in 1942, penniless, disgraced and, most importantly, unable to harm anyone any more.

ACKNOWLEDGEMENTS

A book like this one is reliant on the hard work and diligent research of many other journalists and writers. I've taken facts from too many stories written by my colleagues and predecessors to list them here, but I do want to acknowledge grateful thanks. And also to admit that even if I slag it off, I'd have been entirely stuffed without the internet.

I did lean on a few sources more heavily than others and am grateful to be able to single them out for special mention now. I'd have got nowhere without Francis Wheen's *How Mumbo-Jumbo Conquered the World*, which was full of superb ideas, as well as countless useful facts. While researching US presidents, I loved reading Mark Singer's *Trump and I*, Hunter S. Thompson's *The Great Shark Hunt* and, inevitably, Christopher Hitchens' *The Trial of Henry Kissinger*. I was also impressed by Andrew J. Bacevich's *The Limits of Power*. As I noted, I found many of my *Daily Mail* facts in a superb *New Statesman* article written by Peter Wilby in 2014. I first realised that Henry Ford didn't invent half so much as we credit him for thanks to Carlton Reid's fine book about cycling, *Roads Were Not Built for*

Cars. I first encountered the term 'wanker-magnet' in relation to Ayn Rand on a brilliant blog called *The Age of Uncertainty* (http://ageofuncertainty.blogspot.co.uk). The story of John Romulus Brinkley is told so well in the Gimlet Media podcast Man of the People that I was left roaring with laughter and gasping for air. I read an awful lot of Milton and Rose Friedman's *Free to Choose*. Afterwards, Naomi Klein's *The Shock Doctrine* clearly and angrily showed where all that nonsense took us. Dennis Johnson of Melville House Publishers gave me some fascinating quotes about Jeff Bezos – not to mention a burning sense of injustice. Talking of Bezos, I'd also highly recommend Brad Stone's *The Everything Store*.

I also want to thank my patient wife and daughter, my wonderful agent Susan Smith and my inspiring editor Zoe Berville.